"You're dead sir," one of the two enlisted men explained. *"That's probably the reason you always feel cold. You've probably been dead all this time and we just didn't detect it."*

The 'late' Doc Daneeka is confronted by his own mortality and the insanity of life in Catch 22

HEART OF FOOTBALL

David McVay

Reid Publishing

Reid Publishing
53 Church Gate,
Loughborough,
Leicestershire, LE11 1UE
Tel: 01509 856133
Email: mcvay55@fsmail.net

ISBN: 978-0-9558807-0-4

Printed and bound by Cromwell Press
Typeset by Andrew Searle
Cover Design by Tony Rose

For Debby, Tom and Jess - and Mary, Mary

Acknowledgements

My thanks are due to Tony Rose, Mick Holland, Carolyn Maginnis, The Football League, Steve Mitchell, Richard Prime, John Vickers, David Lowndes, James Maggs, Martin Willetts, Henry Winter and Andy Searle. And the sub-editors at the *Daily Telegraph*, who fall into two camps: those who cut copy with tender, loving, care and those who just lopped off swathes from the bottom when they'd had enough and last orders was fast approaching in pubs down the Buckingham Palace Road.

Contents

Foreword

by Henry Winter of *The Daily Telegraph*

IT WAS when Barry Fry started ranting about clowns and circuses after an 11-goal thriller at Barnet, when the Crewe Alexandra goalkeeper grabbed a future England right-back by the throat and members of the 92 Club got lost on the way from the station that I began to suspect I had found the *Heart of Football.*

This daft, sun-drenched day was August 17, 1991, Barnet's debut in the Football League, seemingly a routine, low-key journalistic assignment. Go along. Record the events. Grab a word or two or three with Fry and then file pronto. Six paragraphs, tops.

Underhill was in carnival mood, with Fry rushing around, unloading programmes from his car, geeing up the team, and doubtless planning how to explain to the missus that he would re-mortgage the family home to keep Barnet going. Stan Flashman, ticket tout and serial sacker of Fry, lurked in the background, listening to the turnstiles clicking and thinking of the money generated by 5,090 punters. Not even Charles Dickens could have dreamed up so many extraordinary characters.

In the age before SatNav, Barnet had players based in Gateshead (Kenny Lowe), Bradford (Paul Showler) and Spike Carter (Runcorn). They travelled hundreds of miles for every game, because they wanted to play for Fry, for Barnet, to have a shot at the big leagues. This was John Bull meets Bull Durham.

So they took on Crewe, before a packed press bench, and it was utterly bonkers. Barnet seemed to have won promotion to the Football League but forgotten to have brought their defence with them. At the break Fry's men were 3-2 behind, which was decent enough. The only person in a rage coming off the pitch was Dean Greygoose, who had a glove around the throat of his right-back, Rob Jones, soon to sign for Liverpool and hurtle towards international recognition. From escaping a Greygoose to joining the Three Lions in less than a year. Only in the *Heart of Football*.

With Jones giving little indication of international promise, and every other defender similarly hopeless, the match finished 7-4 to Crewe. Fry, never shy when microphones pass by, launched into a tirade about the game. "The circus was in town today and we were the clowns," he shouted.

The *Heart of Football* beat strong: Fry in his eloquent element, players performing for the love of it, supporters helping behind the bar one minute, sharing jokes out on the terraces the next. Such scenes were played out across the country that day, and continue to be.

Real football people inhabit this realm, a world that the elite experience only on Cup days. Manchester United visiting a fired-up Exeter City. Chelsea heading for a humbling at Barnsley. They witnessed the passion that lies outside the top flight.

At Oakwell, with Barnsley leading with minutes remaining, a little boy sat in the main stand beside himself with excitement that mighty Chelsea were about to be conquered. He held his Bob the Builder lunch-box up in front of his face because he could not bear to watch in case Chelsea threatened an equaliser. When the whistle went, and it was safe to look, he still couldn't see because of the tears of joy blurring his vision.

This is the *Heart of Football*. This is the type of emotion stirred from Oakwell to Underhill and hundreds of stops in between. Some of the best books on football record life below-stairs, works by Garry Nelson, Steve Claridge and David McVay's own hugely filling *Steak Diana Ross*. No one is better placed than McVay to explore the *Heart of Football*.

About the author

David McVay is a former professional footballer who played with Notts County, Peterborough United and, briefly, Lincoln City. He joined the staff of the *Nottingham Evening Post* in 1983 covering his former club, then in the First Division. He spent eight years reporting sport for *The Times* and now writes regularly on lower league football for the *Daily Telegraph*. He has written several books, including a definitive autobiography of Tommy Lawton, which he co-wrote with Andy Smith, about the legendary former England centre forward whose career and life was ravaged by controversy. He also wrote *Steak...Diana Ross*, which was published in 2003, a seminal football tale told through the diaries of a 1970s journeyman player [McVay himself] that became a cult classic. It was selected by *FourFourTwo* magazine as one of the 50 Best Football Books of All Time. More recently, he has penned *Forest Cult Heroes*, detailing some of the finest and most charismatic players to represent Nottingham Forest. Having played against and socialised with several of the book's subjects, it includes his own personal anecdotes as well as recollections from the elite band of players themselves.

Introduction

IT might have been the moment Willie Carlin jumped over the advertising hoarding at The Shay and confronted one of his detractors in the crowd. There was probably only one hoarding that carried advertising at Halifax Town's ground in the early 1970s. Certainly, there was only one Willie Carlin.

But after the bandy-legged midfield anchor had plied his craft in familiarly dogged fashion for Notts County reserves one wet and windy night in Yorkshire, he took offence at a rather crude remark from the terracing and hot-footed it past a couple of startled flat caps and their dogs (they might have been whippets but I wouldn't like to pander to a regional stereotype) and engaged his biggest fan in earnest dialogue, punctuated with coherence but by and large a conversation dedicated to the pleasing alliteration of industrial language.

I think it was then, during that momentary lapse of concentration from the ultimate professional, an inexplicable urge to resist a lifetime of conformity and join the bus bound for the irrational, that I became forever smitten with life in the nether regions of the Football League.

Ever since, it has been part of my working environment as a player and journalist; the vague aroma of badly burnt onions on open grill; the vague notion that the adjacent food might actually have been alive at some time.

Add the lunatic left winger to that, the ragged right back and an all-consuming pong emanating from a shabby toilet block, plumbed by Severn Trent considering the amount of water it's leaking. It may have a limited appeal, but given the chance to witness the outrageous or original and I'd take Edgar Street's crumbling environs and risk a suspect hot dog drowned in mustard any day in preference to the Riverside, Reebok and a half time prawn sandwich.

Carlin's memorable excursion into the terracing came long before Eric Cantona took a shine to kung-fu fighting at Selhurst Park but some years after Frank Large, one of my boyhood heroes then playing as a defender for Kettering Town, decked Roger Connell, a gangling Wimbledon centre forward, before disappearing down the Rockingham Road tunnel without awaiting the referee's disapproving marching orders.

There were no fisticuffs, just several verbal volleys echoing around The Shay that wild evening in Halifax, although the irony that wee Willie, whose venomous Scouse sarcasm could reduce fellow professionals to jelly and tears, should 'take offence' at a throwaway barb from a local yokel was not lost on colleagues.

If history has a repetitive side, the sight of Dennis Wise wailing on the verge blubbering in the Gillingham press room in September last year about a referee's insulting behaviour towards him [he used the naughty 'f' word when addressing little Den, known as Wisey to his Leeds chairman Ken Bates] induced similar incredulous hilarity amongst anyone in earshot.

Like the Carlin moment, there have been others too. Defining ones that enforce your feeling of warmth to the theatre of football acted out at its less salubrious venues.

Apart from the backdrop, anything from a slag heap to verdant pastures or, at old Gay Meadow, a park and the River Severn, what makes the drama so intoxicating is the cocktail of impulsive youth, aspiring unknowns and veterans of the bigger stage, once illustrious performers under the bright lights, now coming to terms with floodlight failures and the darkly comedic twilight of their careers.

A mixture of *Crossroads*, the motel soap, of which someone once pronounced that the faulty wooden props displayed more movement and inspired more emotion than the cast ever could, and Gielgud and Olivier reminiscing on tour at the Bangor Hippodrome, life in the lower leagues was, and remains, a fascinating reflection of the human condition.

Ian Botham registering on my defensive radar while he was wallowing around the Old Showground for Scunthorpe reserves springs to mind, although in fairness 'Beefy' was by then well on the way to acquiring the sort of Boys' Own status that his Ashes series against Australia bestowed upon him in 1981.

Then there was the lingering, hushed fallout of Billy Bremner's deathly post-match implosion in the home team dressing room at Belle Vue.

Bremner was not a heroic figure in the McVay psyche but, as with most of his Leeds contemporaries, he had burgeoned a deserved respect by virtue of brusque endeavour and a natural talent.

Thus, when he kicked me once at Elland Road, it felt more like a privilege than a metal stud embedded in the back of the left leg. Like a Bavarian swordsman nurturing a duelling scar on the cheek, or a lovelorn teenager's forelocks touched by David Cassidy's roadie's best mate, it was several days before I washed the damaged area, which I would have proudly exhibited to the world, or at least in my local pub, had it not been against the law to drop your trousers in public places back then, even on Hampstead Heath.

A few years later, as a Hull City player, he was too slow to inflict serious wounds on opponents either, although his creative skills were still evident. But it was as Doncaster Rovers manager where he comprehensively dismantled an entire football team with a viperous tongue that simultaneously torched the paint off the walls when Bremner's international pedigree finally collided with the limitations of Fourth Division fodder.

In truth, his Doncaster side had battered Peterborough United that day but somehow, even with myself at right back, we emerged with a 4-0 victory that defied any amount of logic. None of which prevented the former Scotland and Leeds captain extracting the equivalent of Shylock's pound of flesh from the souls and self-respect of the poor sods gathered, presumably with heads bowed, next door to our own away team dressing room that was also hushed, for entirely different reasons.

During my playing career, incidents like those and characters, both on and off the pitch, were regarded as occupational hazards. Dotty directors, potty players and supporters deserving to be certified, by their own admission mostly, just for following their team so slavishly. In short, the lower leagues, the Third and Fourth divisions in pre-Premiership currency, were breeding grounds for eccentrics, rogues and mavericks who in a parallel universe might have spent much of the time in a padded cell inside a very safe and secure institute.

So when asked years later by the *Daily Telegraph* to go and report on the asylum's progress, the answer was as swift and as positive as a Roger Federer backhand.

Call me a grumpy old man, embittered old pro. Or perhaps call me plain old-fashioned but when a former president of a country whose authorities send out a warrant for his arrest takes over a football club, that is stretching brand loyalty to a limit. When that same team then employs a dull Swede and more foreign names than you would hear bandied about on a Loughborough building site, it becomes a Blue Moon too far.

Next step Robert Mugabe buys Sheffield Wednesday?

"I'm Wednesday till I die," they may chant up in the steel city, but if you get in touch with the right despot, that finality bit can probably be arranged for Tuesday.

Put it like this, given the freedom of choice of being stuck in a elevator for five minutes with Dagenham chairman Dave Andrews, a former Great Britain and England amateur international, or Thaksin Shinawatra, a former prime minister of Thailand, then there really is only one decision to be made. Tea and biscuits in the Daggers' clubhouse with chairman Dave.

So I should be grateful to Wee Willie, Big Botham and Bonnie Billy, wee though he was as well, for their moments.

They provided me with a glaring insight and unshakeable faith. For when is it that you realise that your world is a mad place but that maybe it is better to be one of the inmates? Because when the real world intrudes, one that is inhabited by politicians, speed cameras and Piers Morgan, suddenly life becomes very scary indeed.

And a lot less funny and bonkers.

Tranmere Rovers 1 Leeds United 2

Prenton Park

*Minus-15 in Leeds was the gloating weather report
as the punished West Yorkshire club made their league debut
at Tranmere and their inaugural appearance in the third tier
of our domestic game.*

IT is amazing how tetchily Leeds United folk have reacted to accusations that they have been bending the rules. Given previous form, neutrals might have thought any slight on the club's reputation should have been water off a duck's back.

On his first of 44 days in charge at Elland Road in 1974, Brian Clough demanded that the reigning English champions consign their medals to the dustbin because they were a bunch of 'cheats'.

In the context of such malpractice, failure to conform to insolvency policy may seem a trifling matter, but then when the protagonist happens to be Leeds chairman Ken Bates, the only wonder was how so many of the remaining 71 Football League club chairmen were not trampled to death in the stampede last week to re-affirm their 15-points deduction imposed as punishment.

That is three less and counting down thanks to this 2-1 victory over Tranmere Rovers at Prenton Park, the first league meeting between the pair and Leeds' debut in the third tier of domestic football. Bottom of League One, but it's only minus-12 over Leeds today.

Chris Greenacre deservedly side-footed Rovers ahead before a set-piece, fittingly of 1970s vintage, saw Matt Heath swivel from the defensive wall and head a 55th minute equaliser. Tresor Kandol supplied the winner – in front of 2,000 travelling fans – late on as Tranmere turned their backs on a throw-in, an offence that once merited a firing squad at dawn for professional footballers.

"It feels like we were knifed in the gut. We were naïve and we end up being mugged," Ronnie Moore concluded with some justification after the Tranmere manager was the subject of some terrace abuse from home fans following some late substitutions. "There are a lot of very talented managers in the stand, aren't there? Shuker was battered black and blue, Leeds got away with blue murder. Some of their players would have been locked up on a Saturday night for some of the tackles."

Moore is not the first manager in football history to question the physicality of a robust Leeds side. He is unlikely to be the last either.

Yet for all Clough's rage at blatant misconduct and careless whispers from within by 'Careless Hands' Gary Sprake, the Welsh goalkeeper who dropped a few clangers on the pitch and a few bombshells off it with allegations that Revie attempted to buy results, there is a dichotomy at Elland Road. They were a great side, despite the obsessive, dossier-driven Revie, and in defeat they could also be magnanimous. After the carrot-crunching yokels of Notts County beat the then European Cup finalists of the previous season, Bremner, Reaney *et al*, in a League Cup tie at Elland Road, it was Norman Hunter who greeted us from behind the players' bar with a bottle of beer and congratulations, though probably through gritted teeth.

Hunter's team was one whose bite was far worse than its bark. Riding good fortune at Prenton Park, the current Leeds seem to rely heavily on the chihuahua yappings of manager Dennis Wise.

At the final whistle, the players whooped and hollered and cuddled in a huddle in the centre circle where Gus Poyet, Wise's assistant, dived in on top. Their fans were even more ecstatic than the Uruguayan. Yet not a title won nor a cup in sight. Never mind.

Siege mentality had been successfully restored. Them and us, Leeds against the rest of the world. How Revie would have approved.

Tranmere Rovers (4-4-2): Coyne; Stockdale, Chorley, Goodison, Sherriff; Shuker (Curran 83), McLaren, Jennings, Davies; Greenacre (Taylor 81), Zola.
Subs: Tremarco, Kay, Achterberg (g).
Booked: Stockdale, Chorley, Goodison.
Goal: Greenacre (22).

Leeds United (4-4-2): Ankergren; Richardson, Marques, Heath, Lewis; Weston (Flo 76), Hughes, Thompson, Westlake; Beckford (Howson 90), Kandol.
Subs: Carole, Parker, Elliott.
Booked: Beckford, Kandol, Thompson, Westlake.
Goals: Heath (55), Kandol (89).

Referee: L Mason (Lancashire).

POSTSCRIPT: *Late goals and winning matches became indelible features as the season unfolded for Leeds, who quickly moved out of arrears and into the black after nine successive victories. After Poyet was tempted to join Tottenham Hotspur, Wise eventually left for Newcastle United as director of football. Apparently Kevin Keegan was not consulted on the appointment.*

Saturday, August 18

Dagenham and Redbridge 2
Wycombe Wanderers 2

Victoria Ground

After two defeats in their first two games, the newcomers go in search of their first victory in this, their inaugural season in the Football League.

TELEPHONE numbers can reveal an awful lot about the cut of person's jib.

At Dagenham and Redbridge, they have retained the normal land line version, as opposed to those jolly expensive and time-consuming premium rate digits preferred by veterans of the Football League and television production companies offering banal prizes already past their sell-by date.

At their Victoria Road ground, renamed the London Borough of Barking and Dagenham Stadium to highlight the partnership between sport and politics, the connection by Bakerlite or mobile is as rapid and direct as the Thames Estuary English that greets callers.

As the club celebrated its first home game in League Two, the accents and perceived wisdom from the indigenous gathering flowed almost as fast as the action as Wycombe Wanderers rallied to claim a point in an entertaining 2-2 draw that denied Dagenham a historic victory.

"The three most useless things: parking wardens, bailiffs and referees," claimed one of the local wags, that is in the old sense of the expression, one of whom even Roy Keane might approve rather than the plastic-laden variety that adorn our national footballers. Darren Deadman, who had earlier refused Daggers a decent penalty shout, had just pointed to the spot after Danny Foster's careless challenge on Sergio Torres in time added on.

Jermaine Easter converted to cement a recovery begun by Matt Bloomfield's header, thus negating Chris Moore's finish and Sam Sloma's 33rd minute goal, Dagenham's first in the Football League.

In the sponsor's area, emotions were delicately perched, but Ted Hardy was conspicuous by his placidity.

'Father Ted', as he is known by some, has managed Dagenham on three separate occasions and guided them to Wembley as many times as amateurs and semi-professionals. A lifetime vice-president, the 78-year-old former Arsenal reserve team player is confident the young element that current manager John Still has cultivated will survive in this inaugural league season.

Nearly 600 Wycombe fans swelled the attendance to 2,280, but at least hope springs eternal since the club often embrace disaffected migrants from Tottenham Hotspur and West Ham United. Business is expected to be brisk once winter sets in.

Brisker than the double-decker that conked out at Sandbach services following defeat at Stockport County the previous Saturday. Russell Powis, the supporters' club secretary, was one of 83 travelling Daggers followers stranded. He returned home at quarter-to-four the following morning, optimism undiminished naturally, when a replacement finally turned up in Cheshire at midnight.

"It seems as if our big day just won't come," he noted with a shrug after this defeat.

Adversity is nothing new to Dagenham, however, having been denied League status by Boston United's contract irregularities (2002) and Doncaster's 'golden goal' in the Conference play-off final (2003, the rule scrapped the following year).

A police control box, without a side window to view the main entrance, CCTV cameras and electronic counters on the turnstiles are the main concessions to League entry. The other was to become a limited company yet, although their members' club status has been lost, chairman Dave Andrews has ensured that the ten-man committee remain in charge.

"We were proud of our members' status and no one man can take control of the club, everything has to go to a vote," he said. A former Great Britain and England amateur international, Andrews played for Walthamstow Avenue and Leytonstone, two clubs that gradually merged and are part of the hybrid, along with Redbridge Forest, that saw the modern club formed in 1992.

On the weekend that a bust of Sir Alf Ramsey, Dagenham's most famous sporting son, was commissioned for Wembley, Andrews received a medal from the FA in honour of 50 years service to football since he was an 18-year-old.

Keeping faith with those services, he has been known to dodge boardroom banter and enjoy a half-time cuppa in the social down below, discussing events of the first 45 minutes.

"People start to talk stocks and shares and I'm afraid that's just not me."

You can be sure that when Dagenham talk in terms of gate money and wages, they don't talk in telephone numbers either. It's a fine tradition they may care to cherish and observe whatever level of football they enjoy.

Dagenham and Redbridge (3-5-2): Roberts; Uddin, Boardman, Griffiths; Foster, Saunders, Southam, Huke, Sloma (Graham 74); Nurse (Strevens 37), Moore (Taylor 72).
Subs: Thompson (g), Okuonghae.
Booked: Foster, Strevene.
Goals: Sloma (33), Moore (49).

Wycombe Wanderers (4-4-2): Shearer; Martin, Christon, McCracken, Johnson; Bloomfield, Holt, Boucaud (Bullock 53), Oakes (Torres 53); Easter, McGleish (Sutton 67).
Subs: Young (g), Stockley.
Booked: none.
Goals: Bloomfield (69), Easter (90, pen).

Referee: D Deadman (Cambridgeshire).

POSTSCRIPT: *Dagenham did not have to wait long for a first league win, beating Lincoln City at home a fortnight later. Still favourites for a swift return to their previous level, the Conference champions seemed on course to fulfil the turf accountants' prediction until a spectacular five-match winning sequence in February and March, scoring 15 goals and conceding only three, provided a vital safety cushion. Wycombe improved to claim a play-off place but found Stockport, who were eventually promoted, a bridge too far.*

Saturday, August 25

Brentford 2 Barnet 1

Griffin Park

One of England's great defensive warriors, often bloodied but unbowed, gets to grips with galvanising a club with modest ambitions but a fantastic location where a pub greets every corner flag on the rustic old ground.

IT has been an auspicious start for Terry Butcher at Brentford. His first three games in charge at Griffin Park have yielded five points and the team relegated last season remain unbeaten this time around.

"Solid without being spectacular" is how he described it, almost the perfect epitaph for his sterling work as an England centre-half two decades ago.

There is even better news. His wife Rita's ticket was picked out to win the 50-50 raffle draw recently and she promptly donated the £100 prize to club funds, an amount that virtually paid the food bill for Brentford's playing staff last week.

As a token of appreciation, Dave Carter, the kit man and gourmet chef, known as 'Disco Delia', bought a bunch of flowers for Mrs Butcher.

"I didn't mention who they were from, I just gave her them from myself," laughed Butcher, before heading home for a glass of his best Rioja with Rita.

Far from undernourished, then, but imbued with the necessary hunger of aspiring youth and lower league ambition, Brentford secured a dogged 2-1 win over Barnet in the Saturday heatwave near Kew Bridge.

It was Butcher's first win as a manager in England since his Second Division Sunderland side beat West Bromwich Albion at Roker Park in September 1993. A month later he departed after a 2-0 home defeat by Southend.

The theme of red and white stripes should continue more harmoniously at Brentford and, funnily enough, another red obsession emerged during the match as referee Paul Melin sent off Lee Thorpe, on his Brentford debut after serving a three-match ban carried over from his Torquay days, for a nasty tackle on Max Porter.

Reduced to ten men, Charlie Ide's impersonation of a Frank Bruno opponent hitting the canvas earned the home side a penalty, converted by Kevin O'Connor. Jason Puncheon, rated by his manager Paul Fairclough as 'Premiership class', levelled with a fittingly scorching shot on the hour before Melin's meddling saw Stevland Angus dismissed for holding back Ryan Peters and another controversial penalty awarded. Lee Harrison saved O'Connor's effort this time before John Mousinho finished from the rebound.

Enough column inches have been devoted to their calamitous deficiencies recently, but fair to say Melin, who showed three players red officiating at Cheltenham two weeks ago, is best not to hold his breath awaiting a bouquet of flowers and a thank you note from either manager this week.

At clubs such as Brentford, seemingly impervious to the modern age, and dreamily wedged in a time warp between terraced housing and genuinely local pubs, the search for a family atmosphere is but a short journey.

The Princess Royal public house, first left out of the main entrance and a few yards down at the corner of Braemar Road, is a decent substitute for married folk whose spouses 'just don't understand them'.

Butcher recognises the family unit as an essential ingredient so implicit in his formative years at Ipswich Town.

He has also installed 12 new faces, including five loan players, on a minimal budget. Three of this back four at the weekend were under 20 years of age, not quite as young as the roof that finally, after years of eager but frustrating anticipation, appeared on the Ealing Road stand this summer.

There's also a different name on the New Road Stand this season. Not Greg Dyke, the chairman, nor indeed Rod Stewart, the celebrity pop star who once had trials with the club. It's named after Bill Axbey, a lifelong supporter who lived just a few yards behind it who died earlier this year, a few weeks shy of his 103rd birthday.

Now that's what you call keeping it in the family.

Brentford (4-4-2): Hamer; Starosta, Osborne, Mackie, Basey; Mousinho, Pettigrew, Moore, Ide (Peters 58); O'Connor (Poole 85), Thorpe.
Subs: Brown (g), Smith, Pead.
Booked: none.
Sent off: Thorpe.
Goals: O'Connor (50, pen), Mousinho (71)

Barnet (4-4-2): Harrison; Hendon, Burton (O'Ceaurill 48), Angus, Nicolau; Puncheon, Porter, Leary (Hart 20) (Hatch 72), Seanla; Thomas, Birchall.
Subs: Graziou, Beckwith (g).
Booked: none.
Sent off: Angus.
Goal: Puncheon (61).

Referee: P Melin (Surrey).

POSTSCRIPT: *Solidity turned into vapidity, in terms of the Brentford team at any rate. Terry Butcher was sacked in December just as Barnet were overcoming Burton Albion in an FA Cup replay at Underhill. By the end of the season, only a point, in Barnet's favour, separated them in mid-table.*

Saturday, September 1

Hartlepool United 4 Oldham Athletic 1

Victoria Park

*Newly-promoted Hartlepool entertained
newly-released Lee Hughes.*

NOT since Eric Cantona was on the brink of making his Leeds United debut at Boundary Park have the press corps laid siege with such intensity to Oldham Athletic.

Fortunately, Cantona was not around in Hartlepool this weekend discussing trawlers and sardines. Legend has it they don't take to kindly to washed-up, incoherent French impressionists in these parts.

Cantona's arrival in Oldham, and England, was 15 years ago. Roy Butterworth, Oldham fan man and boy and pioneer of Radio Latics in 1963 when steam ruled the railways and airwaves, remembers that a record 66 media staff, 12 from Paris, were somehow housed. "Not without its problems," he recalled. But then it should have been a doddle for a club that accommodated Ken Bates' ego during its embryonic stages as fledgling chairman.

Still, Cantona's first coming has been eclipsed by the media interest provoked by the Lancashire club's decision to offer Lee Hughes a job following his recent release from Featherstone Prison.

Hughes had served half of a six-year sentence imposed after his Mercedes car had been in collision with a Renault in November, 2003, killing one the passengers and severely injuring the driver. Hughes fled the accident and handed himself in to police 36 hours later.

Last week, there was nowhere to run or hide. Looking pale and gaunt and acutely ill at ease in an unfamiliar role, he endured a torrid time at a press conference to reiterate his contrition and attempts to move on with his life.

It was very similar for Hughes at Victoria Park on Saturday as Hartlepool United trounced his team 4-1 to move third top in League One and demote Oldham, play-off semi-finalists last season, into the relegation places.

Whatever the moral issues, and there are many, Hughes enjoyed the vocal support of the travelling fans, who somehow chanted his name in between devouring a relentless supply of meat pies and chips.

Their more predictable focus of attention, aside from the North East gastronomy drenched in tomato sauce, was the referee, who was blameless in their side's abject failure even after Craig Davies had punished Godwin Antwi's early error. Ian Moore restored parity in seconds, James Brown nudged Hartlepool ahead and Richie Barker, after Sean Gregan's clumsy challenge, added a third from the penalty spot before half-time.

Danny Wilson, the Hartlepool manager, thought Hughes might be 'rusty' after his three-year stretch away from the game he last played competitively for West Bromwich Albion as they celebrated promotion to the Premiership, despite a 2-0 home defeat to Nottingham Forest on May 9, 2004.

Andy Liddell's swarthy summer tan did indeed resemble the colour of rust, a stark contrast to the shaven Hughes, whose blanched features suggested he's spent the last few months in the company of a Transylvanian count rather than fellow category C inmates.

He fluffed his solitary chance, a decent one, wide on the hour, much to the delight of Hartlepool supporters who had booed his every touch. In that respect, their vocal chords were not exhausted. Joel Porter's finish confirmed the superiority of last season's League Two runners-up.

After his warm-down Hughes declined to be interviewed. In the Durham sunshine, at least only the seagulls were hovering and not the vultures.

Hartlepool United (4-4-2): Budtz; McCunnie, Nelson, Antwi, Elliott; Brown (Porter 64), Liddle, Sweeney (Humphreys 37), Monkhouse (Foley 76); Moore, Barker
Subs: Lee-Barrett (g), Clark.
Booked: none.
Goals: Moore (16), Brown (26), Barker (44, pen), Porter (84).

Oldham Athletic (4-4-2): Crossley; Eardley, Thompson (Trotman 53), Gregan, Bertrand; Liddell (Wolfenden 53), McDonald, Kalala (Allott 53), Taylor; Davies, Hughes
Subs: Pogliacomi (g), Lomax.
Booked: Kalala, McDonald.
Goal: Davies (15).

Referee: R Shoebridge (Derbyshire).

POSTSCRIPT: *Hughes' rehabilitation continued at Boundary Park, where he scored eight goals before the end of the season. The victims and their relatives of his actions five years ago may not care too much.*

Sunday, September 9

Wycombe Wanderers 1 Brentford 0

Adams Park

Protesters gather in one corner of England that will, they hope, be forever upstanding.

THE uninitiated might have expected smoke signals to hover above the Hypnos Terrace at Adams Park yesterday.

Like a persecuted minority, a section of Wycombe fans and a smattering of others from nearly 30 clubs around the country, chose the League Two game with Brentford to present their case for being allowed to stand during the course of a football match.

Strangely enough, the designated area is sponsored by bed manufacturers Hypnos, who normally prefer their clients horizontal not vertical. At least events on the pitch did not induce slumber as the visiting team, reduced to ten men in the second half when Sammy Moore was sent off for second yellow card, succumbed to a late penalty converted by Jermaine Easter, who has been drafted into the Wales squad for the European qualifier with Slovakia on Wednesday.

Victory eased any pressure that Wycombe manager Paul Lambert might have felt, but Brentford's failure to secure three points deprived Terry Butcher's young charges of the chance of sharing top spot.

The protest passed safely as intended in trying to persuade the top two tiers of clubs to include similar spaces where supporters can indulge themselves in the traditional manner almost extinct in the game today.

The rallying cry is not for a return to the pre-Taylor Report days and wholesale terracing, more of freedom of choice in the current nanny state culture.

The crucial moment arrived in the 80th minute as Martin Bullock dummied his way into the 18-yard area where Grant Basey's ill-advised lunge from behind felled the former Barnsley player.

Smack in front of the Hypnos Terrace, no doubt Wycombe fans had a few words of advice to dispense to the hapless defender. "Should have stayed on your feet, mate," they might have told the Brentford left back.

Wycombe Wanderers (4-4-2): Young; Martin, McCracken, Johnson, Stockley; Bullock, Bloomfield, Holt (Oakes 68), Williams (Torres 46); McGleish (Sutton 68), Easter.
Subs: Shearer (g), Reid.
Booked: Johnson, Stockley.
Goal: Easter (81 pen).

Brentford (4-4-2): Hamer; Starosta, Osborne, Heywood, Basey; Moore, Pettigrew, O'Connor, Poole (Connell 79); Shakes, Ide (Pead 69).
Subs: Brown (g), Smith, Mousinho.
Booked: Hamer, Moore, Basey.
Sent off: Moore.

Referee: A Hall (West Midlands).

Saturday, September 15

Mansfield Town 1 Chesterfield 3

Field Mill

Old enemies, both political and sporting, draw swords in North Nottinghamshire's Robin Hood territory.

THERE was a high noon showdown at Field Mill on Saturday, although it used to be late on Friday night when Mansfield most resembled the Wild West.

As the last chip shop in town closed its doors, the streets echoed to the sound of bare knuckle on cobblestones as fight night began its painful but inevitable journey to the nearest A&E department.

If the old market place is far quieter these days, then the visit of Chesterfield guarantees to stir passions.

Never mind the natural enmity of cross-border rivalry, this fixture is spiced with vitriol steeped in historical and political diversity.

When Margaret Thatcher crushed the unions and decimated the national coal industry during the 1984 Miners' Strike, Nottinghamshire colliers continued to work. In Derbyshire they downed tools. Thus two mining communities were divided irrevocably.

Clad in darkest blue on Saturday, Chesterfield swamped Mansfield 3-1 like the thick blue line of policemen that dispersed flying pickets during the conflict two decades ago.

From the moment Gregor Robertson's third minute corner drifted into the net, the visiting fans were taunting their familiar 'scabs' chant. They were silenced briefly by Stephen Dawson's superlative volleyed response, fortunately with his left foot. The midfield player might have damaged the pink varnish that was discovered on his right toenails before the defeat at Peterborough the previous week, a result of 'messing around with his girlfriend the night before!' Allegedly.

The polish, though, belonged to Chesterfield. Jamie Lowry restored their lead with a tap-in and Jack Lester secured second spot in League Two with a solo injury-time finish, his sixth goal in as many games.

Mansfield, who are third bottom, claimed goalkeeper Barry Roche should have seen red instead of yellow when his cynical 58th minute foul outside the penalty area felled Micky Boulding. The latter, however, twice shot feebly when an equaliser beckoned in the second half.

Even so, it was not the boys in blue, or indeed the man in black, that fuelled Mansfield ire. More the silent hombre in the expensive suit who stood throughout the game on the fringes of the directors' box.

It was 14 years ago that Keith Haslam rode into the frontier town of Mansfield and bought the club. Now the locals want to drive the managing director out, a campaign that has endured three years.

Ugly scenes followed Chesterfield's third goal as fans confronted Haslam, standing just a few feet away, with industrial language more Johnny Rotten than John Wayne.

Right: The Last Post is observed immaculately as Keith Buxton from the Thoresby Colliery Band sounds a moving tribute to Private Damian Wright, from Mansfield, and Private Ben Ford, from Chesterfield, who were killed fighting on patrol in Afghanistan's Helmand Province earlier that month. Chesterfield manager Lee Richardson said: "Events like this certainly put a football match into context." Only an imbecile would disagree.

Pic courtesy of Richard Parkes

James Derry, the Mansfield chairman appointed by Haslam, is trying to buy the club from the current owner, who will then lease the ground back to the new consortium. It's complicated. "You wonder when you see that abuse today whether it's worth taking it on," Derry said. "Everyone in football has a shelf life. He seems to have rather outlived his." The last stagecoach left Mansfield at midnight on Sunday. Haslam was not aboard. Deep in Robin Hood country, Stags fans will be anything but merry men this morning.

Mansfield Town (4-4-2): Muggleton; Mullins, Buxton, McIntosh, Jellyman; Hamshaw, McAllister (Sleath 66), Dawson, Bullock; McAliskey (Holmes 81), Boulding
Subs: White (g), Martin, Wood.
Booked: Dawson, Buxton, McAllister.
Sent off: Buxton. Goal: Dawson (9).

Chesterfield (4-4-2): Roche; Picken, Gray (Downes 62), Kovacs, Robertson; Lowry (Rooney 62), Niven, Winter, Leven (O'Hare 83); Fletcher, Lester.
Subs: Algar, Jackson.
Booked: Lowry, Winter, Roche, Downes.
Goals: Robertson, Lowry, Lester.

Referee: K Friend (Leicestershire).

POSTSCRIPT: *There was talk that Chesterfield's relatively large investment in players and wages would guarantee automatic promotion, but as it turned out they failed even to make the play-offs despite Rotherham's points deduction, which opened up another place at the top. Mansfield's woes, of course, were only just beginning...*

Saturday, September 22

Leyton Orient 2 Hartlepool United 4

Brisbane Road

*The capital's surprising and unfancied league leaders
entertain some surprising and unfancied promotion
chasers from the North East*

AT Brentford, they can claim to be surrounded by pubs.
Across London to the east, Leyton Orient are under siege
from rather more substantial liquid assets.

Instead of sinking pints in every corner, or reds and
heavyweight contenders as Orient chairman and boxing and
snooker impresario Barry Hearn might prefer, the League
One club sold off a quartet of plots into which investors sunk
foundations. Apartment blocks, for sale or rent, have since
blossomed.

The windfall has financed redevelopment on two sides of
the ground, leaving only the old main stand to be preserved
with dignity for the present.

In the meantime, home owners or tenants in this E10
quadrangle have the option of Sky Sports in the front room
every Saturday afternoon or, once a fortnight, Orient live
from balcony. In an unstable housing market, it is
impossible to gauge the effect on property prices but had a
football neutral been visiting at the weekend, the
entertainment alone certainly devalued some of the
highly-hyped and glossy detached products available in the
Premier League.

Like £10 Poms from another era, several residents bathed in deckchairs and autumn sunshine overlooking not Sydney Harbour but Brisbane Road as the home side relinquished their unbeaten league record to Hartlepool United, but not their top-of-the-table status.

Odds on either of these two sides being first and third at this stage would have been long at the start of the season, yet Hartlepool's merited 4-2 victory suggests that Danny Wilson's squad might sustain a second successive promotion.

A blunder by Orient goalkeeper Stuart Nelson allowed Ian Moore to pounce and that lead should have been far greater in a first half punctuated by an uncharacteristically heated debate on the touchline led by Wilson.

Apparently, he was unhappy with the performance of tardy ballboys, a bit like a snooker referee fumbling to re-spot a colour and unsettling the rhythm of Jimmy White in full 'Whirlwind' mode.

Wilson need not have fretted. James Brown added a second when Nelson was exposed by an uneven bounce, JJ Melligan [John James] thundered a response in-off the crossbar before Andy Monkhouse restored the two-goal cushion in the 83rd minute. Substitute Charlie Daniels did make a late half-volley count, an effort eclipsed as Moore finished accurately in injury time.

Even so, Orient's progression from relegation dodgers has been as impressive as the new build, especially as manager Martin Ling has melded 11 new players into a decent unit.

"Top of the league, you're having a laugh" was the taunt from Pools supporters. Ling wasn't smiling, but at least his players remain in pole position.

As for the neighbours, there was always the anticipation of *EastEnders Omnibus* in the front room on Sunday. If that doesn't inspire a rapid return to the balcony in replica Orient shirts, nothing will.

Leyton Orient (4-4-2): Nelson; Terry (Demetriou 61), Thelwell, Mkandawire, Palmer; Melligan, Chambers, Thornton, Corden (Daniels 66); Gray (Echanomi 72), Boyd.
Subs: Morris (g), Oji.
Booked: Thornton, Mkandawire.
Goals: Melligan (57) Daniels (87).

Hartlepool United (4-4-2); Budtz; McCunnie, Nelson, Antwi, Humphreys; Monkhouse, Boland (Clarke 81), Liddle, Brown (Porter 73); Barker (Mackay 90), Moore.
Subs: Elliott, Lee-Barratt (g).
Booked: Monkhouse, Moore.
Goals: Moore (10, 90), Brown (52), Monkhouse (83).

Referee: M Haywood (West Yorkshire).

POSTSCRIPT: *As many predicted, Orient were unable to sustain their good form and drifted away from the promotion candidates, finishing well down the pecking order in 14th position, one place and six points ahead of Hartlepool in fact.*

Saturday, September 29

Gillingham 1 Leeds United 1

Priestfield Stadium

*The winning habit that has become second nature to Leeds
is not expected to be disrupted by lowly Gillingham*

INCONGRUOUS as his nasal tones might have sounded amid
the Medway mayhem, it was impossible to suppress the
thought of Kenneth Williams delivering his classic one-liner
on behalf of Leeds United on Saturday.

"Infamy, infamy," the camp thespian shrieked in *Carry on
Cleo.* "They've all got it infamy."

Instead, and in a turn up for the book, Dennis Wise
expressed his chagrin at being verbally abused by a match
official as the Leeds manager saw his League One side's
unblemished winning start to the season ended in a
smashing 1-1 draw with Gillingham at Priestfield
Stadium.

Forty years to the weekend when their talismanic captain
Billy Bremner was suspended for 28 days for swearing at a
referee, a novel reversal of sorts reveals an enduring but
fractious relationship between Leeds and the football
authorities.

As if being docked 15 points by the Football League wasn't
enough, Leeds suffered further reductions imposed by
referee Danny McDermid as their forward pairing of Tresor
Kandol and Jermaine Beckford were sent off either side of
half-time.

An incandescent Wise, who was also dismissed for rebuking McDermid at the interval, intends to have the man in the black punished for his later alleged comments.

"When a referee tells a manager to 'eff off', it's not acceptable," claimed Wise. "I will be reporting him."

Wise insists he has three independent witnesses, ironically a trio of security guards that were required to escort McDermid off the pitch as the dimwits among the travelling Leeds supporters gathered to gnarl their own obscenities, barricaded in one corner of the ground by stewards and police dogs.

As an alternative form of baiting, the Leeds supporters took perverse pleasure in barracking Gillingham chairman Paul Scally, regarded as something of an anti-Christ back at Elland Road, and definitely one of those who has it 'infaleeds'.

"I think they were friends," laughed Scally, who says he has been the target of some unfair criticism from his Leeds counterpart Ken Bates. "It's pathetic. It's also underhand and outrageous. He [Bates] needs to have a good look at himself.

"I was one of the 60 or so chairmen who asked questions of the two Leeds representatives [when they were punished by committee], but if the Leeds fans would only half listen, it wasn't about them but the people who got them into that mess."

Initially, things had been going so swimmingly for Wise. His arrival on the touchline from the directors' box coincided with Sebastien Carole's headed opener in the 28th minute.

The puerile behaviour demonstrated by Kandol and Beckford, dissent, mocking the referee and playing on to waste time, was the architect of their premature departures. Yet as Gillingham laid siege to the nine men, it seemed midnight might strike before their players scored until Ian Cox headed a deserved equaliser in time added on.

A good result for caretaker-managers Mick Docherty and Iffy Onuora, although Scally is confident a permanent appointment will be made this week.

"I thought the referee made some very brave decisions and he was absolutely spot on" was Scally's verdict. "Referees are under pressure not to make those decisions really and he did superbly. I went to the referee's room afterwards and told him so."

You can almost feel the replica Scallywag dolls being diced by needles and pins in West Yorkshire.

Gillingham (4-4-2): Royce; Clohessy, Sodje, Cox, Hamilton (Dickson 70); Cogan, Lomas (Mulligan 60), Nowland, Crofts; Facey, Graham
Subs: Stillie (g), King, Stone.
Booked: Nowland, Cox.
Goal: Cox (90).

Leeds United (4-4-2): Ankergren; Richardson, Marques, Heath, Clapham (Huntington 57); Prutton, Douglas, Hughes (Westlake 58), Carole (Weston 74); Beckford, Kandol.
Subs: Thompson, Lucas (g).
Booked: Hughes, Kandol, Beckford, Douglas, Ankergren.
Sent off: Kandol, Beckford.
Goal: Carole (28).

Referee: D McDermid (London).

POSTSCRIPT: *Danny McDermid was cleared of all charges by the FA, who banned Wise from the touchline for three games for his behaviour at Priestfield. The engaging Scally appointed Mark Stimson, formerly of Stevenage Borough, as his manager shortly after but relegation awaited his first season in charge.*

Sunday, October 7

Chester City 3 Shrewsbury Town 1

Deva Stadium

Sunday, bloody Sunday and sweet FA arrive at Chester.

THOSE who continue to wage the losing battle to preserve the sanctity of Sunday would have been dismayed at events at the Deva Stadium yesterday.

At a time of day when heritage once dictated that people were strolling out of their local church, or applying the finishing touches to a freshly-waxed Vauxhall Cavalier, a few thousand were flocking to pay homage to a League Two fixture strictly for the converted.

A somewhat exaggerated police presence and the sound of tills preparing to jingle around the adjacent retail park confirmed the worst fears for anyone expecting a traditional day of peace.

Fitting that Shrewsbury Town should be in opposition. Back in Shropshire, their old Gay Meadow ground was demolished at the weekend, eliciting nostalgic remorse that another idiosyncratic football venue has succumbed, like Sunday, to financial pressure.

At least for over an hour, the goalkeepers of Chester City and Shrewsbury Town appeared sympathetic to the notion of observing some quiet and cogitative tranquillity on the Sabbath.

But then a typically frenetic derby induced a rash of comic capers and a veritable epidemic of goals, four of them in 12 minutes, as Chester climbed into League Two's last available automatic promotion place with a 3-1 victory over last season's play-off finalists.

Chester manager Bobby Williamson had cautioned against the noon start, instigated by the police as well as an all-ticket restriction, an imposition lamented by the club who saw what passes for a local derby gate reduced by around 1,000. "It's only bloody fourth division," bemoaned one of the Deva office workers.

Indeed, there was precious little to recommend the game above that level until Richie Partridge got his head down and set off on a run that ended with a smashing 20-yard finish into the top corner in the 62nd minute.

Yet when old boy Darren Moss headed an equaliser seven minutes later, a dismal run of two consecutive defeats seemed destined to end for the visitors.

That was optimism not based on the defensive strategy employed by Kelvin Langmead and Neil Ashton, who, in trying to clear the same ball, clattered into each like a pair of dodgems with *Titanic* skipper Edward John Smith on remote control.

John Murphy was the suitably predatory recipient with a second goal, as was substitute Simon Yeo, who ambled into vacant space at the centre of the back four to volley a third and complete a third win in eight days during a busy schedule of five games in a fortnight.

"You look at that game and everyone is saying it was a brilliant performance," Shrewsbury manager Gary Peters said, talking about England's win over Australia in the Rugby World Cup on Saturday when Stirling Mortlock missed a late penalty chance to seize victory for the antipodeans. "But if the Australians had kicked that last goal, would everyone feel the same way? People would see it in a different light. It's exactly the same here because people will remember the defensive mistakes which killed us."

Another Sunday and another sermon from the press box pulpit lacking in credibility.

Chester City (4-4-2): Danby; Marples, Butler, Linwood, Wilson; Partridge ((McManus 83), Dinning, Hughes, Sandwith (Yeo 62); Murphy, Ellison
Subs: Palethorpe (g), McManus, Rutherford, Holroyd.
Booked: Dinning, Hughes .
Goals: Partridge (62), Murphy (72), Yeo (74).

Shrewsbury Town (4-4-2): Garner; Moss, Kempson, Langmead, Murdock (Pugh 46; Ryan 75); Herd, Drummond, Hunt, Ashton; Symes (Nicholson 81), Hibbert.
Subs: Hall, Esson (g).
Booked: Drummond, Murdock, Symes:
Goal: Moss (69).

Referee: C Foy (Merseyside).

POSTSCRIPT: *Chester's surge up the table was only matched by their plunge down it after Christmas. After a sequence of one win in 14 games, Bobby Williamson was dismissed in early March. A day later, Gary Peters left Shrewsbury by 'mutual consent'. Funny old game.*

Sunday, October 14

MK Dons 4 Lincoln City 0

stadium:mk

Sky cameras pay a return visit to MK Dons at their latest venue for a rematch of the televised fixture that so entertained at the National Hockey Stadium last season.

A VIVID reminder that *'fings ain't wot they used t'be'* bombarded sunny Buckinghamshire yesterday.

In part, that cockney refrain laments wholesale demolition and disappearing landmarks, something they could never be accused of in Milton Keynes where, for the past four decades, the preference has been for an expeditious knocking up of houses, ice rinks and shopping arcades rather than knocking them down.

Perhaps only here could the fitting arrival of an Ikea superstore encourage the local football club to uproot from its temporary residence for new premises across town and around twenty million traffic islands.

The construction of a huge Marks and Spencer on this retail park plot will further assist development, and the completion of the upper tier which remains nakedly deprived of its plush seating.

Two years ago, they opened up Ikea with an Abba tribute band and live reindeers, slightly different from a pair of scissors, red tape and some stuffy civic dignitaries that declared the new town project officially up and running in 1967.

Progress for MK Dons has also been dramatic since its summer relocation from the National Hockey Stadium as the largest crowd in their short history, 13,037, saw them thrash Lincoln City 4-0 and extend their lead at the top of League Two. A first demolition in Milton Keynes perhaps?

Dons manager Paul Ince has cautioned about premature optimism, but the vibes yesterday were mostly positive.

A flowing move, with Dons captain Keith Andrews pivotal, released Leon Knight to open the scoring as half-time approached at stadium:mk, a lower case identity popularly championed by country singer kd lang.

Just a few moments earlier, Oliver Ryan's clumsy first touch ruined his chance to steer Lincoln ahead, a recurring theme for the youngster and Lincoln, who seemed as likely to score as the Dons' subs reaching the other side of the pitch pedalling languidly on their static training bicycles adjacent to their dugout.

Unsurprisingly, when Lloyd Dyer added a second in the 70th minute, the visiting team wilted alarmingly in front of Sky Sports.

Last season, this fixture enticed the same cameras on a cold January night when Lincoln were unfortunate to depart with just a point in a riveting 2-2 draw, en route to their fifth consecutive failure in the play-offs.

The statistics reveal the side has won just two games this year, however, and languishing next to bottom, manager John Schofield's position is precarious at best.

A flat back-four with a flat-pack store next door was ominous enough, but the former nowhere near as fiendishly complicated to unravel as the mysteries of the Swedish furniture manufacturer's pine products.

Aaron Wilbraham finished for 3-0 and then Knight completed the rout with a low left foot shot. Played in by substitute Bally Smart, just one vowel away from a famous ringmaster, the circus, with Lincoln in clown disguise, had finally come to town.

MK Dons (4-4-2): Gueret; Diallo, O'Hanlon, Swailes, Lewington (Smart 80); Stirling (Wright 63), Andrews, Navarro, Dyer; Wilbraham (Johnson 86), Knight
Subs: Cameron, Abbey (g).
Booked: Stirling.
Goals: Knight (45, 82), Dyer (70), Wilbraham (78).

Lincoln City (4-4-2): Marriott; Amoo, Bencherif, Brown, Beevers; Frecklington, Kerr, Hand (Forrester 73), N'Guessan; Stallard (Torpey 58), Ryan (Warlow 58)
Subs: Dodds, Green.
Booked: none.

Referee: R Shoebridge (Derbyshire).

POSTSCRIPT: *After steering Lincoln to the play-offs the previous season, where they were soundly beaten by Bristol Rovers in the semi finals, John Schofield was sacked the next day. Cruel game at times, football.*

Saturday, October 20

Hereford United 0 MK Dons 1

Edgar Street

Promotion hopefuls with historic pasts look to the future and the top of the table at an antiquated venue.

IN a parallel universe, or at least with the help of an HG Wells contraption, this fixture could stir the emotions to gladiatorial levels.

A divot on the pitch tees up Ronnie Radford to arrow a searing shot towards the top corner, only for Tellytubby goalie Dickie Guy to defy gravity and his frame to save.

Indeed, both Hereford United and MK Dons, or Wimbledon in their previous incarnation, can reflect on derring-do and FA Cup glory when giants were put to the sword and mercilessly slain.

These days, the only blood shed at Edgar Street emanates from the adjacent cattle market, but at least the defiance of a home side depleted to ten men was commendable before a late Mark Wright volley secured a 1-0 victory, a ninth win in succession for the Dons, who extended their cushion at the top of League Two.

Time machines are not required to evoke the past at Edgar Street where the 'bookend' stands behind each goalmouth resemble temporary shelters for *Stig of the Dump* hosting a dinner party for a platoon of eco-warriors.

Progress may be protracted, but new plans to regenerate the area include a renovation for the old place that has been

Sean O'Hanlon and Theo Robinson tangle for possession.

Pic courtesy of the Hereford Times

home since 1924. Chairman and manager Graham Turner has also presided over an upward spiral since regaining league status two years ago. They remain in a play-off position despite the defeat and despite a slightly patronising credit in the Dons' programme the previous Sunday, a reference to the club being unable to climb much further up the league ladder, which clearly irked Turner as he saw Lincoln City battered 4-0.

Perhaps it was pinned on the dressing room wall to inspire Hereford, but their cause suffered appreciably when Steve Guinan was dismissed seconds before half-time. In his profile, Guinan admits that his other job ambition would be a Formula One driver and his collision with Lloyd Dyer, reckless and ruthlessly premeditated, certainly had the Michael Schumacher stamp of approval.

"He [Guinan] was caught out," Turner admitted. "It was cynical and it goes on in the game and we don't condone it but it was a yellow card. I was staggered when he [the referee] produced a red."

On the day Hereford embraced the anti-racism theme that football is championing, Paul Melin demonstrated a Henry Ford-determination to promote colour. *"You can have the card in any colour - as long as it's red"* seems to be the Surrey

A precious opening in a tight game saw John McCombe's header galvanise MK Dons goalkeepers Willie Gueret into a rare save.

Pic courtesy of the Hereford Times

official's slogan. He has now ordered off seven players in eight games this season. Just four to go and he can start on his second XI...

Hereford United (4-4-2): Brown; McClenahan, McCombe, Broadhurst, Taylor (S Johnson 90); Ainsworth (Webb 71), Smith (Benjamin 90), Diagouraga, Easton; Robinson, Guinan.
Subs: Ingham (g), Rose.
Sent off: Guinan.

MK Dons (4-4-2): Gueret; Diallo, O'Hanlon, Swailes, Lewington; Wright, Navarro (Cameron 84), Andrews, Dyer (Smart 76); Wilbraham, Knight (J Johnson 64)
Subs: Broughton, Abbey (g).
Goal: Wright (87).

Referee: P Melin (Surrey).

POSTSCRIPT: *Since Edgar Street's fate and plans to move to new premises are in the hands of the local council, no one will be surprised to hear that few are holding their breath in Hereford awaiting news of renovation. When last heard, Paul Melin's yellow card total had reached 51 - but not for a single game apparently.*

Saturday, October 27

Darlington 0 Chesterfield 0

Darlington Arena

Even David Tennant, in his guise as Dr Who, might struggle to fathom the mystery of time and space that has been landed upon County Durham.

PERHAPS it was a fear of enclosed spaces that persuaded George Reynolds to uproot Darlington from Feethams four years ago.

Certainly, visiting players to the picturesque ground who had to endure a post-match communal wash in a rustic concrete tub know how Jo Brand and Jennifer Saunders might feel should the lardy laughter-makers share a bird bath next charity relief day.

Reynolds, the former Darlington owner and safe-cracker now generally reviled in town, eventually did end up serving time in a confined space – a prison cell – for tax evasion. But not before he had guided the County Durham club, assisted by the local council, to their present home, the Darlington Arena, whose prefix changes according to the highest sponsorship bidder.

Further proof that this was a case of the blind leading blind faith emerged on Saturday as just under 3,500 home fans in the 4,205 crowd were swamped inside the 25,000 capacity stadium during their team's 0-0 draw with League Two promotion rivals Chesterfield.

It is not the first time that politicians motivated by vanity and a misplaced sense of their own importance have been persuaded by deluded visionaries that bricks and mortars will convert the masses and attract admirers in their droves. Witness the Millennium Dome.

The historic Reynolds, Balfour Webnet, Williamson Motors, 96.6TFM stadium/arena (in no particular chronology) goes beyond the sublime as a folly, however. As much as it is impressive and luxurious, its current capacity has been trimmed to 10,000 because the infrastructure can scarcely support even that sort of crowd, a glaring oversight by Reynolds given his past vocation demanded that decent access and swift getaways were priorities when planning ahead.

In the Reynolds dream, Darlington were supposed to eclipse Sunderland at their Stadium of Light. As Harry Clarke, a former Darlington footballer and Durham cricketer from the 1930s, once famously remarked: "It's looking a bit black over Bill's mother's."

If the good people of Darlington deserve better, and they do, at least the team under Dave Penney is doing its best. The manager may feel obliged to ask potential acquisitions if they have a history of agoraphobia in the family, but high profile signings Julian Joachim and Pawel Abbott were absent for more football related injuries as Darlington toiled in front of goal while maintaining their unbeaten start at home to the season, their fifth in the new location.

Cardiff's on-loan forward Matt Green, more Matt Amber given his uncertainty – and certainly not Matt Finish, was profligate on two vital occasions and suffered sporadic abuse, although on the plus side, he could have identified his detractors with ease in the stands and maybe noted their mobiles for further frank exchanges.

Jamie Ward's left-foot effort, saved by David Stockdale, replacing Andy Oakes who sustained a hip problem in the warm-up, was as close as Chesterfield came to the win.

The present owners are boasting about more development and more multi-purpose sport complexes. A ten-pin bowling alley and indoor ski-dome have been discussed. It must be difficult for Darlington to contain its euphoria.

Darlington (4-4-2): Stockdale; Austin, White, Foster, Purdie; Colbeck, Ravenhill, Keltie, Smith (Cummins 59); Green (McBride 90), Blundell.
Subs: Miller, Brooks-Meade (g), Brackstone.
Booked: Ravenhill

Chesterfield (4-4-2): Roche; Picken, Kovacs, Downes, Robertson; Lowry, Niven, Leven, Bastians; Lester (Rooney 81), Ward
Subs: O'Hare, Gray, Winter, Allison.
Booked: Picken.

Referee: S Attlwell (Warwickshire).

POSTSCRIPT: *Darlington partially justified some of their pre-season big-spending by reaching the play-offs, where they were edged out by Rochdale, 5-4 on penalties after the scores were tied at 3-3 in the second leg.*

Tuesday, October 30

Nottingham Forest 0 Oldham Athletic 0

City Ground

Most managers insist that there is no such thing as a bogey side. Oldham have the chance to contest that opinion on the south bank of the River Trent.

COLIN CALDERWOOD discovered last night that when it comes to expectations, nothing should be taken for granted where Nottingham Forest are concerned.

The Forest manager had anticipated a maximum nine points from three consecutive home games, beginning with this one against Oldham Athletic.

But the contest between last season's losers in the play-off semi-finals transpired to be a frustrating affair as the home side failed to secure the win that would have hoisted them to second position and an automatic promotion place.

The Forest programme may have recalled their 1990 League Cup final victory over Oldham in the twilight years of the Brian Clough era but the Lancashire club has proved something of a nemesis recently. Defeat at Boundary Park two years ago ended Gary Megson's tenure, while Oldham scored seven without reply in two matches last season, including a 5-0 festive drubbing that, curiously, inspired a city centre binge drinking party by several of the Forest squad a few days later.

A dismal defeat at Luton Town on Saturday elicited a reality check for Forest and this insipid draw against a side which dragged themselves out of the bottom four by virtue of this point might further erode confidence.

A long range effort by Curtis Davies, tipped over by Forest goalkeeper Paul Smith, was the best of a sterile first half and it was the visitors who posed the greater menace after the interval as Gary McDonald twice was denied by Smith when the Oldham midfielder should have been more decisive in his finish.

The arrival of substitute Arron Davies, on his first appearance since signing from Yeovil in the summer, finally galvanised the Forest cause. His right foot volley flashed narrowly wide, then some neat footwork created an opening that Chris Cohen, under pressure, was unable to convert.

The same combination returned shortly after and once more with a similar result, this time Cohen's profligacy with a weak left foot stab at the ball being less excusable.

Nottingham Forest (4-3-3): Smith; Chambers, Breckin, Wilson, Bennett; Clingan, McGugan (Thornhill 85), Cohen; Holt (Davies 63), Agogo, Commons.
Subs: Morgan, Power, Roberts (g).

Oldham Athletic (4-4-2): Beresford; Eardley, Trotman, Stam, Betrand; Liddell, Kilkenny (Allott 90), McDonald, Taylor; Wolfenden (Smalley 69), Davies
Subs: Ricketts, Kalala, Crossley (g).

Referee: M Haywood (West Yorkshire).

Saturday, November 3

Carlisle United 3 Leeds United 1

Brunton Park

*Leeds United's unbeaten start in the league, 13 games
and counting, faces a test of nerve and character
at a club striving for the top.*

JORDAN Carrigan wore a troubled expression during the
half time interval at Brunton Park. Not one to compare with
a Martin Jol frown, Kevin Keegan fret or Martin O'Neill
implosion, the like of which tend to get either the Samaritans
motivated or stir the UXB squad into action.

Elevated from announcing results over the Tannoy to
preparing tea and coffee for Radio Cumbria at the back of the
main stand, young Carrigan's worry line served only to raise
his appearance to primary school level rather than reveal his
actual age of 13 years.

"I had a funny feeling about this game," he said as the
kettle boiled limply on a painful go-slow that mirrored
Carlisle United's first-half efforts against Leeds United.

He was not alone. Just a few yards away, Eddie Gray, the
former Leeds winger and manager, signed autographs
between working for Yorkshire local radio. He, too, had been
cautious about this match, although not quite as
apprehensive as one of his previous visits to the ground, 33
years to the month in the old First Division.

Leeds, defending champions of England, had survived 44
days of Brian Clough, but a trip to Carlisle, who fleetingly

had occupied the top berth often reserved for their feted visitors, was a trip into the unknown.

However, true to an Elland Road tradition that is observed religiously even today, Leeds were battered for 90 minutes but prevailed when a late Duncan McKenzie shot floated into the net to secure a 2-1 victory.

Yet, when Jermaine Beckford guided a left-foot shot past Carlisle goalkeeper Kieren Westwood in the 28th minute, the need for a composed Leeds side to rely upon the last-minute antics that have been proved so productive for them this season seemed wholly unnecessary.

Out of the muddle of mediocrity, though, Carlisle fortunes were revived when a hopeless Marc Bridge-Wilkinson free kick was cleared to Simon Hackney, who executed an unerring 25-yard volley to level just after the hour.

"That [the abject free-kick] just about summed up my day," admitted a candid Bridge-Wilkinson, omitting that in fact he was pivotal in two later goals that carried Carlisle to a 3-1 win and the top of League One, while curtailing Leeds' unblemished start to the season.

The diminutive midfielder's centre from a short corner allowed Joe Garner to head a second at the near post and in the time added on, normally the witching hour for Leeds to reap rewards, he dummied two defenders from another short corner and finished from a tight angle to calm home tensions among the capacity 16,668 crowd.

Last April, many of them stayed behind to applaud Bristol City off the pitch, even after the champions-elect had effectively ended their own play-off aspirations, and Carlisle folk once more offered a gracious handclap to the departing side. In the coach park behind the Waterworks End, some of the 3,400 Leeds fans were throwing stones, a barbaric ritual which most civilised countries long ago abandoned.

Never mind. Leeds manager Dennis Wise was magnanimous in defeat and Jordan Carrigan's perplexed look had vanished. That 'funny feeling' had turned into an ecstatic one as he jigged to the beat of *'We are top of the league...'*

One suspects football purists will share his moment of pleasure.

Carlisle United (4-4-2): Westwood; Raven, Livesey, Murphy, Aranalde; Anyinsah (Gall 72), Lumdson, Bridge-Wilkinson, Hackney; Garner, Graham
Subs: Arnison, Smith, Howarth (g).
Booked: Bridge-Wilkinson.
Goals: Hackney (61), Garner (70), Bridge-Wilkinson (90).

Leeds United (4-4-2): Ankergren; Richardson, Marques, Heath, Clapham (Huntington 90); Prutton (Constantine 76), Douglas, Hughes, Carole (Da Costa 77); Kandol, Beckford.
Subs: Weston, Lucas (g).
Booked: Clapham, Prutton, Heath, Hughes, Kandol.
Goal: Beckford (28).

Referee: P Dowd (Staffordshire).

Saturday, November 10

FA Cup first round

Barrow 1 Bournemouth 1

Holker Street

The Cumbrian chill greets fans and players alike from the South Coast with the scent of FA Cup upset in the breeze.

THE FA CUP knockout factor is likely to take on added significance when these two teams meet at Dean Court next week. Defeat for either manager is certain to signal the end of their tenure.

Kevin Bond, whose Bournemouth side languish third bottom in League One, had a smile for the hardy fans who had set off at 6am to see Jem Karacan's left foot effort in first half stoppage time steal an undeserved draw after Kevin Rapley's opener had raised hopes of Barrow's first victory over league opposition in this competition for 40 years.

"I couldn't see where Bournemouth would score after that," admitted John Bond, Kevin's dad, who was present to support his son at a fittingly windswept Holker Street, a chilly Cumbrian venue avoided by Darren Anderton whose 'hamstring strain' sick note excused him travelling from the south coast.

Bond senior was picked up by the team coach near Manchester and he thought his son's side had 'gotten out of gaol'. Still, the prospect of relegation lingers over Bournemouth, as does that of redundancy over Bond junior.

The Blue Square North club also have demotion issues that were not evident as former Liverpool academy defender Steve McNulty towered above all others.

Phil Wilson refused to discuss his own precarious position. Now his players must take time off work for the replay. At least the roads around Leigh may be a little safer then.

"My order book will empty for a couple of days," said Rapley, once of Reading and now a driving instructor, whose finish secured his first goal for the club since his move from Leigh RMI last month. A lesson in precision three-point turning to all his pupils.

"Bournemouth knew they had been in a game and it showed. There's no reason why we can't go down there and do it again. This is a bit different from teaching pupils how to drive but I don't mind taking the time off and neither will the rest of the lads."

Barrow (4-4-2): Deasy; Woodyatt, McNulty, Jones, Butler; Henney, Sheridan, Bond, Brown; Rapley, Rogan (Thompson 79).
Subs: Wilson, Elderton, Bayliss, Archer (g).
Booked: Henney, Sheridan.
Goal: Rapley (19).

Bournemouth (4-4-2): Moss; Telfer, Cooper, Gowling, Pearce; Pitman (McQuiod 78), Karacan, Hollands, Goldbourne; Vokes, Kuffour.
Subs: Stewart (g), Partington, Bartley, Newman.
Booked: Gowling.
Goal: Karacan (45).

Referee: M Haywood (Yorkshire).

POSTSCRIPT: *Barrow's achievement did not curry favour with the board, who sacked Phil Wilson on the following Tuesday, a week before the replay. It took a penalty in time added on for Bournemouth to rescue the tie after Barrow had led 2-1, and there was further heartache for the part-timers as a Matty Hollands goal in the last minute of extra time knocked them out of the competition. The consolation was a remarkable revival, which peaked when Barrow defeated Stalybridge Celtic 1-0 in the divisional play-off final to secure a place in the Blue Square Premier. Millwall did for Bournemouth in the next round and it took a ten-points deduction for entering administration to galvanise Bond's side into recovery mode, too little, too late as it transpired.*

Saturday, November 17

Walsall 0 Luton Town 0

Banks's Stadium

*Luton Town seek solace in the Black Country at the end
of a week when the club found themselves accused
of serious wrong-going by the FA.*

SOME call them parasites, others, like Sam Allardyce and Sir
Alex Ferguson, call them son. Whatever the disparate
opinion, there is no doubt that you can't keep a good, bad or
distinctly ugly agent down these days.

Luton Town are the latest club to be accused by the FA of
wrong-doing involving payments to agents, one of whom is
called Sky Andrew, innocent of all charges perhaps but
definitely guilty of retaining a name that suggests he may
have been fostered by Bob Geldof and Madonna in a previous
life.

Throw in a troubled board and an anxious former
chairman and the Mad Hatters' Tea Party should benefit
from an Eric Morecambe entrance, a surreal appearance in
one of those famous festive plays 'wot' was written by his
hairy-legged associate Ernie Wise.

Asked what he thought of it so far as the club drew 0-0
with Walsall at the Banks's Stadium, Luton's most celebrated
supporter is certain to have shrieked 'Rubbish' from the
comic hall of fame beyond the grave.

In fact, if any of the 55 charges brought against the League
One club, some of its directors, its old chairman Bill Tomlins

and a variety of agents should stick, the FA might consider a sentence of 100 uninterrupted hours viewing repeats of this guileless epic in solitary.

In between gruel and water rations, the guilty parties may be inspired by Tommy Mooney's snap second-half shot smothered by Luton goalkeeper Dean Brill, while a glaring miss by Michael Ricketts, a former England centre-forward who once commanded a £3.5million transfer fee from Bolton Wanderers to Middlesbrough, is certain to comfort confined agents, a cheery reminder of how much money can be made from mediocrity in their industry.

Currently, there is little to cheer Luton manager Kevin Blackwell. A local lad who once plied his trade as a builder while shoring up a dodgy Boston United back four as goalkeeper, returning to his hometown club should have a fitting reward for a honest and respected professional who has survived working shifts with Neil Warnock and Ken Bates.

Instead, Luton are in turmoil. Former manager Mike Newell, the self-styled champion against illegal bungs, says the FA's stance has 'vindicated' his criticism of Luton and the bungs culture.

Less justifiable, though, is a series of extended contracts granted to several players past their pensionable age (35 in football years) as the club slid hopelessly towards relegation last season. It left Blackwell with a clutch of players earning around £200,000 a year, a staggering amount for a club in the old third division, and in particular goalkeeper Marlon Beresford, who will be 41 when his contract expires.

Not content with that fiscal curiosity, Newell, who was eventually sacked, is taking the club to court for a reported £3million, an amount that would bankrupt Luton and force them into administration.

The fear is that the FA, since the Stevens Report failed to finger any culprits at Premier League level, will make an example of the minnows. In which case they may care to paraphrase Eric Morecambe's classic rebuke in their defence.

"We were paying all the right notes," he almost said, tugging on Andre Previn's lapels. "But not necessarily in the right order sunshine."

Walsall (4-4-2): Ince; Weston, Gerrard, Dann, Fox; Hall (McDermott 63), Sonko, Wrack, Demontagnac (Taundry 83); Ricketts, Mooney. **Subs:** Roper, Bossu (g), Deeney. **Booked:** Gerrard.

Luton Town (4-5-1): Brill; Perry, Coyne, Fojut, Jackson; Bell, Spring, Hutchison, McVeigh (Talbot 70), Wilson; Andrew. **Subs:** Goodall, Currie, Keane, Grant. **Booked:** Perry, Hutchison.

Referee: A Taylor (Greater Manchester) .

Sunday, November 24

Wrexham 2 Chester City 2

Racecourse Ground

Brian Little returns to management at basement club
Wrexham in a week when Steve McClaren's hopes
of a summer in the Swiss Alps, minus his umbrella,
also hit rock bottom against Croatia

THE Racecourse Ground in the North Wales drizzle yesterday was not the place for detractors who recoil at the resumption of the Home Internationals.

Certainly, those who are dismayed by the merest display of national identity and frown upon the virtues of honest toil and controlled aggression would have been forced to turn away in anguish as Wrexham (of Welsh origin) and Chester City (representing England) slugged it out in a belting local derby that ended 2-2.

At least our country's most richly-rewarded failures, i.e. the England football squad and its coaches, might have benefited from compulsory attendance.

While the less savoury headlines suggest that the closest some of the nation's finest are getting to emulating Eastern European technique is by close study of a few poles and the body swerve of women gyrating around them, they may have suffered severe nausea upon seeing how the other half lives down in League Two.

Commitment to the cause and a pride in their work may be alien concepts to the rich and famous in the game today, but they were evident in every tackle and passionate challenge in this rowdy encounter, where physical contact was allowed a rare unbridled outing.

There was also a welcome return to the game for Brian Little, taking charge of Wrexham nine days after his appointment to help out Brian Carey, the former incumbent who has remained at the Racecourse as assistant.

"After five minutes, I was jumping around and moaning and Bobby [Williamson, the Chester manager] shouted across and laughed, 'Welcome back'," said Little, who, 13 years ago to the day, celebrated his 41st birthday by becoming Aston Villa manager.

When Kevin Roberts volleyed an exquisite opener after 26 minutes, it seemed as if Little's 54th birthday bash would be a more muted one as Chester sought to end a sequence of three defeats that has hindered promotion progress.

A few choice words exchanged between Chester's Kevin Allison and a section of home supporters was the prelude to the goal and a source of anger after it as the bald Scouser mimicked his critics.

A wig and some false teeth and voila, shades of *An Audience with Steve McClaren* at the Peckham Hippodrome.

Williamson, a volatile Scot adding spice to the cross-border rivalry, was also less than impressed as Michael Proctor equalised from what may have been an offside position.

Paul Linwood restored the advantage in first-half stoppage with a firm header after a similar effort from Paul Butler had earlier been cleared off the line, although Wrexham's revival merited a second leveller, this time Proctor's extended right foot finishing substitute Matty Done's left-wing centre with a sweet volley in the 75th minute.

Despite the point, Wrexham remain bottom of the pile, fearful of a ruinous relegation that was so narrowly avoided with victory over Boston United on the final day of the season last May.

Little is optimistic – and rightly so. Sporting red shirts, his players looked comfortable in a fluid 3-5-2 formation. Maybe the club should consider a trip abroad as incentive to retain their League status.

A summer skiing trip in the Alps perhaps. Switzerland comes highly recommended, untroubled as it will be by any hooligan element of an English variety at that time of the year…

Wrexham (3-5-3): A Williams; S Evans,
Pejic (Done 66), Hope; Baynes, Aiston (Spender 84),
Roberts (Garrett 78), Llewellyn, Taylor;
E Williams, Proctor.
Subs: Jones (g), G Evans.
Booked: Roberts, Proctor, Baynes.
Goals: Proctor (37, 75).

Chester City (4-5-1): Danby; Marples, Butler, Linwood,
Wilson; Partridge, Hughes, Dinning (Grant 25) (Yeo 67),
Roberts, Ellison; Lowdnes (McManus 52).
Subs: Ward (g), Holroyd.
Booked: Lowdnes, Hughes.
Goals: Roberts (26), Linwood (45).

Referee: K Woolmer (Northamptonshire).

POSTSCRIPT: *Wrexham were unable to raise their game or position. Ironically, their derby rivals sank steadily without trace and almost joined them in the Blue Square equation, a goalless draw with Stockport County in their penultimate game finally assuaged relegation fears after an alarming decline in form.*

Saturday, December 1

FA Cup second round

Notts County 0 Havant and Waterlooville 1

Meadow Lane

Despite accounting for Histon by virtue of a laborious victory and flattering 3-0 scoreline in the first round, Notts County expect further smooth progress against the part-time minnows from Blue Square South.

HE cancelled a business trip to Nepal and flew in from Dubai to be present at his club's finest hour and a half. But Marcus Hackney was not content with merely being there. Defying jet lag, he decamped from his comfy leather chair in the main stand to deliver a rallying cry to the players as they left the pitch following their pre-match warm-up.

If Hackney sounds like a football manager's worst nightmare, a jet-setting chairman intent on meddling in team tactics with a potential for foreign investment, the reality is far more convivial.

"I never get involved in the dressing room," the 35-year-old Havant and Waterlooville chairman confirmed after the Blue Square South side's merited victory over Notts County carried them to the FA Cup third round, eclipsing the defeat of York City last month that secured a second round passage for the first time in their history.

"This was absolutely magnificent," said the enthusiastic Hackney as acting captain Jamie Collins approached him and

Hands on head, who would be a manager when your team is playing as badly as Notts County against the part-timers from Havant.

Pic courtesy Nottingham Evening Post

Lawrie Dudfield finds Brett Poate a stubborn opponent as the Magpies succumb to the non-leaguers.

Pic courtesy Nottingham Evening Post

the travelling directors on the boardroom balcony at Meadow Lane and shook each of their hands in gratitude.

Two nights in a 'posh hotel' near Nottingham and a Friday session at Derby County's training ground had fostered camaraderie, although Havant defended with a tad more resilience than the Premier League stragglers.

County last lost an FA Cup tie at home to non-league opposition in 1959, a 2-1 defeat to Bath City, but a surprise seemed likely as the League Two side's confidence visibly wilted before Tony Taggart scored the decisive goal in the 87th minute, the ball crawling over the line as the substitute fell to ground under Adam Tann's unfair tackle.

"I thought it was going wide," admitted Taggart, a former Brentford YTS, who could have claimed a penalty in that eventuality.

While the purists may well be wishing for a white Christmas, Havant will be dreaming of red, specifically in the form of a Manchester United or Arsenal shirt in their festive stocking, in today's third round draw as the season of goodwill approaches.

"I was born in Hammersmith and live next to the QPR ground but I have always supported Chelsea so I would love to get them next," said the goalscorer who sat on the bench when Farnborough Town played Arsenal in this competition four years ago.

In the event, a trip beyond Malvern and on to the valleys beckons after Havant's number came up against Swansea City, away, in the third round which was drawn after the Harrogate Railway-Mansfield Town tie yesterday afternoon.

Havant manager Shaun Gale described it as 'the best day of his short managerial career' just seven weeks after taking charge at a club formed under merger just nine years ago.

This win was thoroughly deserved as County, who beat Histon at the previous stage but who had lost their last two league games, were booed off the pitch by their meagre support of just over 3,500.

Collins, captain on the day replacing the suspended Tom Jordan, summed up the team's emotions: "This is the highlight of my career and we did it for the board. They have been fantastic."

In contrast, Havant's players ran towards their 261 travelling fans celebrating behind the goal where Taggart's crucial strike had trickled over the line after he had been tripped by County captain Tann inside the 18-yard area.

The penalty was not required, however, leaving manager Gale to lavish praise on his charges.

**Another one bites the dust as Neil MacKenzie rues
a rare missed opportunity for the home team.**

Pic courtesy Nottingham Evening Post

"You can have all the money in the world but you can't buy that feeling when the ball went into the back of the net," said the 38-year-old Gale, a former Barnet and Exeter player who was appointed following Iain Baird's departure.

"We did our homework on County and I watched a DVD of them. The pressure was on them and I felt they were there for the taking after half-time."

His opposite number Ian McParland has been at the helm of County a week less than Gale. "A financial disaster" was how he expressed elimination.

It could get worse for the oldest league club in the world. For now, though, the weekend belonged to one of the newest in the non-league sector.

Notts County (4-4-2): Pilkington; Canoville, Tann, Hunt, Mayo; Silk (Lee 60), Mackenzie (Butcher 78), Somner, Weston (Weir-Daley 63).
Subs: Sandercombe (g), Pearce.
Booked: Somner.

Havant and Waterlooville (4-4-2): Scriven; Gregory, Smith, Sharp, Poate; Markin, Oatway (Wilkinson 46), Collins, Potter (Gurney 90); Baptiste, Pacquette (Taggart 49)
Subs: Taylor (g), Warner.
Booked: Taggart, Gurney, Collins.
Goal: Taggart (87).

Referee: J Singh (Middlesex).

The streaker skipper, captain for the day Jamie Collins, can't hide his excitement after Havant's defeat of County - not so much a giant slaying rather a minnow devoured by a tiddler.

Pic courtesy Nottingham Evening Post

POSTSCRIPT: *From the stuff of dreams to a flight of fancy and ultimately a journey into the realms of pure fantasy was how Havant's FA Cup progress was charted. They survived a battering at the Liberty Stadium and escaped with a fortuitous 1-1 draw before thumping Swansea 4-2 in the replay, already knowing that they would be playing Liverpool in the fourth round. They led twice at Anfield, but when Havant eventually pinched themselves, the reality revealed that the Merseysiders had triumphed by the final whistle. But how the memories linger on....*

Saturday, December 8

Notts County 2 Shrewsbury Town 1

Meadow Lane

A week after their humbling FA Cup defeat to Havant and Waterlooville, the Magpies return to the unforgiving and unrelenting struggle to avoid relegation.

IT was Tommy Lawton, one of the few sportsmen for whom the adjective legendary is apposite, who described joining Notts County as one of the worst day's work of his life.

Sixty years ago last month, the enigmatic England centre-forward moved from the fashionable King's Road environs of First Division Chelsea to sign for County, then toiling in Division Three (South). Imagine David Beckham had left Old Trafford for Mansfield Town instead of Real Madrid. That was the shock factor at the epicentre of the deal which established a British record fee of £20,000 in November 1947.

"I should have stayed at Chelsea and transferred the wife," Lawton later reflected after his marriage dissolved in acrimony, swiftly followed by his career.

It is common knowledge the Ian McParland's matrimonial status is harmony personified, but around 3.45pm on Saturday afternoon, he may have been pondering the wisdom of accepting the appointment as County manager eight weeks ago.

A sequence of four successive defeats, including an FA Cup humbling by Havant and Waterlooville, seemed destined to continue after Dave Hibbert's penalty secured Shrewsbury Town the lead at a bleak and barren Meadow Lane.

Worse still, McParland, incandescent with rage at the penalty decision, had been sent off for comments made to the fourth official, doubtless nursing bruised pride and a sore toe bone after launching the sort of right-volley that plundered countless goals during his County playing days against the concrete wall behind his dug out.

Salvation, though, comes in many guises and a mobile phone call to his assistant David Kevan introduced Neil MacKenzie as a second-half substitute. Initially, the impressive centre-half Krystian Pearce, just 17 and on-loan from Birmingham City, levelled with his first League goal, a header after his volley had been well saved by Glynn Garner in the 69th minute. MacKenzie then flighted an immaculate free kick for 2-1 and the victory that raised flagging morale at a club that has slipped into the League Two relegation frame.

It also restored a familiar smile to the face of McParland, known as 'Charlie' by fans when he was a winger here. Performing with an innate passion, he had seen red then, infamously being dismissed seconds after appearing as a substitute in one game against Bristol Rovers; the other red sighting was more pleasing, a cracking 30-yard effort into the top corner that defeated Manchester United in the last seconds of a top flight tussle in 1983.

Raw talent and passion aplenty runs through the McParland veins, but his visage had been grim after his latest dismissal that seemed to capture a career in microcosmic fashion.

He was somewhat optimistically, not to say foolishly, hailed as the 'new Jimmy Sirrel' by his chairman, a member of the supporters' trust that runs the club. A millstone akin to announcing that Colin Calderwood is the 'new Brian Clough'. Only a fans' mentality, perhaps.

Above: Wrong move - Kevin Pilkington guesses incorrectly as Dave Hibbert's penalty claims a deserved lead for Shrewsbury.

Pics courtesy of Dan Westwell

Below: Shirt-lifting Spencer Weir-Daley, formerly a Nottingham Forest trainee, tugs on Darren Moss, the Shrewsbury right back.

Still, McParland's appointment has been a popular one on the north bank of the Trent. As has the return of former players Kevan and Tommy Johnson in the dugout, and with another favourite Dean Yates on duty as a local radio pundit, there is an air of reunion and the old boot-room mentality at Meadow Lane that may yet prevail.

"How's your foot, Charlie?" Yates, once the apprentice who cleaned McParland's boots, asked as the manager prepared to be interviewed. It drew another smile, although more seriously, a lack of goals from his forwards remains a concern.

If only there was another Lawton willing to risk all at the Lane. Mrs Shevchenko denied Harrods and Armani for the Pound Shop in Nottingham's Old Market Square? Now that would be grounds for divorce.

Notts County (4-4-2): Pilkington; Silk, Pearce,
Tann (Canoville 89), Hunt; Dudfield, Butcher,
Somner (MacKenzie 56), McCann;
Lee (Parkinson 61), Weir-Daley.
Subs: Sandercombe (g), Sam.
Booked: Silk.
Goals: Pearce (69), MacKenzie (75).

Shrewsbury Town (3-5-2): Garner; Langmead, Moss,
Murdock (Ashton 85); Herd, Drummond, Hunt, Davies,
Tierney; Hibbert, Symes (Nicholson 66)
Subs: Esson (g), Jones, Hall.
Booked: Herd.
Goal: Hibbert (41, pen).

Referee: N Miller (Durham).

POSTSCRIPT: *County's flirtation with relegation evolved into
a long-running affair that neither party could break off until the
final throes of the season. The supporters' trust continues to
flounder in finding fresh investment and another winter of toil
and trouble looms for long-suffering Magpies. Shrewsbury
could not sustain their play-off exertions of the previous season
and eventually departed company with Gary Peters, the
manager who had guided them out of the Conference.*

Left: Neil MacKenzie celebrates his curling free kick that brought relief
and three points for Notts County with Richard Butcher, the club's
eventual leading scorer by some distance with 12 goals.
Manager Ian McParland had an elevated view of the winner
having been dismissed in the first half .

Pic courtesy of Dan Westwell

Tuesday, December 11

FA Cup second round replay

Barnet 1 Burton Albion 0

Underhill

Son of Brian attempts to venture further in the one competition his famous dad could never master.

GOOD news of progress in Barnet last night. After a lengthy battle with the local council, the League Two club was finally granted permission to redevelop their ground and remain on its current premises.

Better still was their safe FA Cup passage to conclude another protracted saga, this time against Burton Albion, in their second round replay at Underhill.

Extra time loomed when Adam Birchall punished Burton's first defensive error of the evening to convert Jason Puncheon's right wing corner in the 83rd minute.

Two years ago Burton drew Manchester United as their third round prize. Barnet must visit Swindon. So it was not all good news for the Bees.

Without a win in six matches, Barnet scarcely exuded confidence against their Blue Square Premier opponents. Only in the final moments of a simply dire first half did they threaten, but Birchall's shot from a fittingly hoisted pass ended tamely in the side netting.

In fact, it was ten minutes after the interval before the most fluent move of the game emerged, begun in the Barnet half and developed in some style with Birchall's flick releasing Kenny Gillet in the 55th minute.

The full back seemed certain to put neutrals out of their misery with a decisive finish before Kevin Poole's splendid reaction save flipped his left foot effort over the top.

Barnet almost regretted their profligacy five minutes later when Keith Gilroy's faint touch from a long throw bounced off the crossbar to safety.

Both sides adopted a more cavalier approach as the temperature plunged below freezing. Still, the final whistle was a blessed relief all round.

Barnet (4-4-2): Harrison; Devera, Yakubu, O'Cearuill, Gillet (Nicolau 80); Carew, Leary (Porter 72), Bishop, Puncheon; Grazioli (Thomas 80), Birchall.
Subs: Beckwith (g), Hendon.
Goal: Birchall (83).

Burton Albion (4-4-2): Poole; Brayford, Greaves, James, Webster; Corbett, Simpson, McGrath, Gilroy (Stride 85); Edwards, Harrad.
Subs: Goodfellow, Austin, Farrell, Deeney (g).
Booked: McGrath.

Referee: A Woolmer (Northamptonshire).

POSTSCRIPT: *Barnet were eventually undone by Bristol Rovers in the fourth round, while Nigel Clough's Burton were edged out of the Blue Square Premier play-offs by Cambridge United, who eventually lost to Exeter City in the final.*

Saturday, December 15

Peterborough United 1 MK Dons 2

London Road

Top of the division's rich list and top of the league, the leading protagonists meet for League Two's match of the day.

THE Scottish accent was as biting as the chill factor that hovered above the River Nene as he crossed the bridge adjacent to London Road on Saturday. He had travelled south that morning as family ambassador for the game between League Two's heavyweight promotion contenders.

Inside the ground, a first touch was less than encouraging as the father of Colin Cameron saw his son flattened by the flailing arm of a Peterborough United defender with the match barely tepid.

The proud dad need not have fretted. The MK Dons midfield player recovered and helped create his side's second goal as the leaders extended their cushion at the top of the table with a merited 2-1 victory, despite being reduced to ten men for the last 13 minutes of a thoroughly engrossing affair with their closest rivals.

Caledonian cheer was not universal in the Fenlands, however. Sir Alex Ferguson had also journeyed to support his son and fledgling Peterborough manager Darren. But if consolation was among his parental post-match duties, the Manchester United manager also found time to proffer advice to one his old boys.

"Don't start counting until March," former United midfield anchor Paul Ince was told by the real governor of Old Trafford, who then invited the Dons' manager for a glass of wine, perhaps to celebrate an eight-point gap that has emerged between the Dons and the play-off places.

At least Cameron senior was able to witness most of the early jousting and jostling. Before either of Peterborough's prolific forward pairing of Aaron Mclean (18 goals) and Craig Mackail-Smith (13 goals) could muster a finish, the dreaded Health and Safety had already struck, decreeing that some home fans could not sit in their normal seats. Result, chaos and disaffection outside the stadium as hundreds queued after kick-off, less than imbued with the festive spirit.

When finally they joined the 10,351 crowd, they cursed Peterborough's luck when Charlie Lee's effort smashed against the crossbar in a first half shaded by the Posh, but then bemoaned careless defending as Kevin Gallen stole the first goal for Dons and Keith Andrews clipped another, the captain's tenth of the season.

Gallen, Lloyd Dyer and Mark Wright should have ensured it was a formality before McLean's volley, following up another Lee shot that rattled off the bar, raised hopes, heightened after Drissa Diallo was sent off for a second yellow card.

In defeat, an air of optimism lingered around London Road. Certainly, judging from what Ferguson described as a 'proper game of football', both these clubs should be competing at the higher level next season.

Ferguson's relationship with his gregarious chairman, Darragh MacAnthony, appears as convivial as it is constructive. Asked about reports that Charlton Athletic had offered £2m for Mclean, the chairman, whose wealth is derived from his property business, replied with fitting Irish whimsy: "I assume they were talking about his right boot."

The past is prominent at Peterborough, from the Noel Cantwell suite to the memories of FA Cup giant-slayings in their Midland League era. The legacy Ferguson and his employer hope to leave is introducing the Posh to the Premiership. A long-term dream maybe.

But don't discount father and son Fergie crossing swords should it come to fruition.

Peterborough United (4-4-2): Tyler; Gnakpa, Morgan, Blackett, Day; Low (Hughes 64), Lee (Howe 85), Hyde, Boyd; Mackail-Smith, Mclean.
Subs: Jalal (g), Keates, Whelpdale.
Booked: Gnakpa.
Goal: Mclean (75).

MK Dons (4-5-1): Gueret; Diallo, O'Hanlon, Swailes, Lewington; Wright, Navarro Cameron (Johnson 85), Andrews, Dyer (Stirling 71); Gallen (Wilbraham 77).
Subs: Broughton, Abbey (g).
Booked: Diallo.
Sent off: Diallo.
Goals: Gallen (47), Andrews (57).

Referee: N Miller (County Durham).

Saturday, December 22

Luton Town 1 Tranmere Rovers 0

Kenilworth Road

*The season of goodwill is conspicuous by its absence
at Luton as the consequence of its punishment for entering
administration begins to bite with devastating effect.*

THE Salvation Army turned up at Kenilworth Road on
Saturday. The Samaritans would have been more fitting.
That is if Luton Town could have stretched to the phone call.

Docked ten points by the Football League for entering
into administration, then anchored at the foot of the table
last week, there was some respite for manager Kevin
Blackwell's side with a 1-0 victory over Tranmere Rovers
that lifted them a couple of places in League One.

Another Merseyside visit, Liverpool in the third round of
the FA Cup on January 5, offers further hope, but it is a
fleeting reprieve. Luton is a club perilously close to a
permanent mooring at rock bottom.

Blackwell must raise £1.3million by April to satisfy
creditors, but that figure includes players accepting a 50%
reduction in their wages. He has already forfeited his
monthly salary to pay the YTS staff over the festive period.

The latter is perceived as more of a season of badwill at
Luton as the League imposes stiffer and stiffer penalties.
Pivotal central defender Jaroslaw Fojut is among three loan
players who must return to their clubs next month; Luton
have been advised to recall their on-loan players to assist but

two of those, Ahmet Brkovic and Marlon Beresford, earn double the combined monthly salary of the departing trio, thereby compounding Luton's financial woes should they return.

Such fiscal folly is just one of the concerns of chairman David Pinkney, who is remaining stoically at the helm trying to entice new owners. Even so, the vultures are hovering over the Eric Morecambe Suite.

Football agents survive on percentages and they can sniff a large wedge amongst what Blackwell describes as 'bankrupt stock'.

Nottingham Forest have already offered a huge markdown value of £150,000 for David Edwards, who swept the decisive goal over the line after Tranmere goalkeeper Danny Coyne obligingly dropped Matthew Spring's centre at his feet in the 69th minute.

Can it get worse? Probably, although there is one incentive for potential investors. The old ground stands on the site of a redevelopment scheme which would be funded by a £300m grant from European coffers. A hitherto indifferent local council is suddenly more focused on relocating the club to pastures new to expedite matters.

These, though, are peripheral issues to Blackwell, for whom a takeover scarcely promises job security despite recouping £6million in transfer revenue since he was appointed in March.

A sense of déjà vu prevails after his travails with Leeds United and a protracted and on-going libel case with Leeds chairman Ken Bates has exacerbated the burden.

Raising a smile is almost as big an achievement as raising a winning team. Blackwell deserves some Christmas cheer and the goodwill of Luton fans for combining both so seamlessly at the moment.

Luton Town (4-5-1): Brill; Perry, Coyne, Fojut, Goodall; Bell, Edwards, Robinson, Spring, Currie (Talbot 67); Furlong (Andrew 17).
Subs: Keane, McVeigh, Grant.
Booked: Robinson, Fojut, Coyne, Perry.
Goal: Edwards (69).

Tranmere Rovers (4-5-1): Coyne; Stockdale, Goodison, Sherriff, A Taylor; Greenacre (Curran 76), Ahmed (Myrie-Williams 76), Henry, Jennings, Suker; G Taylor.
Subs: Tremarco, Zola, Achterberg (g).
Booked: Greenacre, G Taylor, Goodison, A Taylor.

Referee: T Kettle (Rutland).

Saturday, December 29

Swansea City 3 Leeds United 2

Liberty Stadium

*An eagerly anticipated meeting between the team
who were actually top of the league against the one
whose chairman clings to the belief, through his
programme notes, that they are.*

THE barometer needle that hovers over Swansea City
appears to have been stuck on deep depression for many
years now. For Leeds United, the climate change has been
heading alarmingly in the same direction, a more recent
decline but equally bitter in its bite.

A nostalgic trip in the programme for this game at the
Liberty Stadium on Saturday indicated warmer, more
comforting afternoons when the newly-promoted Welsh
side spanked the then mighty Leeds to announce their
debut in the old First Division 26 years ago in August.

Few at Vetch Field that day can forget such a dramatic
arrival; few in the ground record sell-out crowd of
19,010 at the weekend will forget Swansea's stirring 3-2
victory over their League One promotion rivals either.

If after a fall there comes a rise, then the interim
penance should always be as joyous as this riveting
encounter. Revving up in the fast lane, it refused to pull
over during a breathless contest that saw the home team
reduced to ten men after the 37th minute dismissal of
Ferrie Bodde.

Gary Monk blocks Jermaine Beckford's passage to goal.

Pic courtesy of Huw Evans agency

Now five points clear at the top of the table, Swansea's renaissance has been crafted by their Spanish manager Roberto Martinez.

Torching the holiday homes of the casual English tourist was once the pastime of some raving loony Welsh arsonists but xenophobia is the antithesis of Swansea's doctrine.

After a brief exile in Chester last season, Martinez has returned to the helm and fashioned a cosmopolitan squad brimming with energy and talent. Two Dutchmen and three Spaniards have been introduced, the latter mirroring his own career in England when Wigan owner Dave Whelan bought him and two compatriots to perform as the inevitably dubbed 'Three Amigos' in Lancashire.

Bodde's sobriquet was slightly more sinister and the 'Dutch Roy Keane' certainly didn't shirk from fulfilling it with a terrible lunge on Jonathan Howson that merited a red card for him and a stretcher for his victim.

Get in! Gary Monk's towering header claims the lead for Swansea after trailing to a sloppily conceded Darren Beckford effort.

Pic courtesy of Huw Evans agency

Actually the tackle was more Johnny Giles without the sly disguise, but by then, Andy Robinson's smart free-kick and captain Gary Monk's thumping header had steered Swansea ahead after Jermaine Beckford had punished Dennis Lawrence's lethargy to level.

Leeds' central pairing were also culpable in first-half stoppage time, although there was much to admire in Jason Scotland's unerring surge and finish. When Alan Thompson reduced arrears with another fine free-kick seconds after the interval, home fans feared the worst. A minute later, a similar Thompson set-piece rebounded off the woodwork, an omen that heralded a third defeat of the season for Leeds, who had flown to Cardiff on Friday to prepare for the game.

"I hope the fans are proud of the players," espoused Martinez.

Fair to say ecstatically so. Memo to Fabio Capello?

Swansea City (4-5-1): De Vries; Rangel, Monk, Lawrence, Painter; Anderson (Tate 84), Pratley, Bodde, Britton, Robinson (Butler 74); Scotland (Bauza 69).
Subs: Orlandi, Duffy.
Booked: Monk, Rangel, Robinson.
Sent off: Bodde.
Goals: Robinson (9), Monk (25), Scotland (45).

Leeds United (4-4-2): Ankergen; Richardson, Marques, Heath, Hughes; Howson (Prutton 40), Thompson, Carole (Weston 77), Westlake (Flo 67); Beckford, Kandol.
Subs: Huntington, Kishishev.
Booked: Hughes, Westlake, Heath, Rankin.
Goals: Beckford (12), Thompson (46).

Referee: A Marriner (West Midlands).

Not for the first time, nor indeed the last, Swansea players celebrate a job well done. The 10-men have beaten Leeds in a Liberty thriller.

Pic courtesy of Huw Evans agency

POSTSCRIPT: *From Don Revie to Ken Bates, Leeds have always attracted support and disdain in equally fervent and occasionally repulsive measure. Having flown down the evening before the Swansea game, the squad booked in at a local hotel where the players dined on Friday night. Hearing of their arrival, a local resident took his grandson and huge Leeds fan to the hotel and sat patiently in the reception area for a couple of hours while the team ate their evening meal. Finally relaxing in the comfy chairs of the hotel lounge, the granddad approached a group of four players with his young charge and asked if they would mind signing autographs. "We're too busy, could you go away," came the reply. This from Third Division fodder. With such misplaced arrogance, how could anyone fail to love Leeds United's distinguished players, perfect ambassadors for the lower leagues.*

Tuesday, January 1, 2008

Luton Town 1 Yeovil Town 0

Kenilworth Road

New year, new hope for the Hatters?

THE figure 10 should be uppermost in Luton Town's thoughts currently. The amount of penalty points deducted for entering administration has been recouped in four festive games that ended yesterday with this win over Yeovil Town, who had Paul Warne dismissed a minute from time.

In fact, the score could have reached double figures at Kenilworth Road. Drew Talbot and David Edwards struck the woodwork and countless openings were thwarted by a variety of goalkeeper Steve Mildenhall's anatomy before Calvin Andrew finally stooped to head the winner in the 48th minute.

However, when Jaroslaw Fujot threw his shirt to the crowd to mark his farewell appearance for the Hatters, the on-loan Bolton Wanderers player could not have performed a more fitting finale.

Plunged into a third administration within a decade last November, the League One club may be lucky to emerge with only its back bare as it sinks further into the financial mire.

Even the lucrative FA Cup third round tie at home to Liverpool on Sunday fails to disguise Luton's plight. Crisis does not even begin to reveal the extent of their problems.

Fujot, the imposing Polish defender, misses the Liverpool match having been forced to move back north by Football League rulings, one of three loan players who have returned. As replacements, the League insists that Luton's Ahmet Brkovic (from Millwall) and Dean Morgan (from Southend) should return to Kenilworth Road, even though their combined wages will add a further £4,000 per week to the players' wage bill. The latter has not been paid since October and a meeting with PFA officials is expected to be deferred later this week.

"The whole thing beggar's belief," said exasperated Luton manager Kevin Blackwell. "I don't argue with the ten points we were deducted, but when you are trying to keep a club alive and make it an attractive proposition for buyers, you just don't need any more punishments."

There have been other hindrances for the team fourth from bottom of their division trying to surprise last season's Champions League finalists.

Intervention from the PFA has deprived them of their fitness instructor and several scouts. All overnight stays have been cancelled; last week they turned up at Port Vale 25 minutes before kick-off after being delayed in traffic. Preparations for Sunday have been described as 'low key'.

The possible absence of England midfielder Steven Gerrard with a calf strain for the visitors at least offers some hope for Luton, if not for burglars on Merseyside.

"We could do with a draw then beat them away then draw Man United at home and do the same, all the way to the Final. That might just about solve our current financial problems," Blackwell said. At least a sense of humour remains a low maintenance and un-taxable item out of reach of the Revenue.

The visit of Liverpool for the third round tie will also evoke the number 10 for Luton, who were unable to beat Nottingham Forest's ten men in the 1959 Final at Wembley.

On this form, however, it may be Luton's turn to prevail in adversity.

Luton Town (4-4-2): Brill; Keane, Fojut, Perry, Goodall; Bell, Spring, Edwards, Currie (McVeigh 87); Andrew, Talbot (Furlong 90).
Subs: Hutchison, Jackson, Robinson.
Booked: Spring.
Goal: Andrew (48).

Yeovil Town (4-4-2): Mildenhall; Rose, Forbes, Guyett, Jones; Warne, Way (Owusu 61), Dempsey (Barry 80), Stewart, Stieber (Williams 59); Walker.
Subs: Alcock, Bircham.
Booked: Warne, Stewart, Williams, Rose.
Sent off: Warne.

Referee: D Whitestone (Northamptonshire).

POSTSCRIPT: *Luton basked briefly in a moment of glory when Liverpool scraped a 1-1 draw at Kenilworth Road before easing through to the fourth round with a 5-0 win at Anfield. Kevin Blackwell had despaired about his future and duly found himself out of a job, despite his good track record, when new owners arrived at the club. He replaced Bryan Robson at Sheffield United and took them to within a whisker of the play-offs from an almost impossible position. Finishing bottom was the least of Luton's worries. Before kick-off for the new season, they have already been docked ten points by the Football League for transgressing transfer rules. If that smacks like a sledgehammer cracking a walnut, going to press, a further 15 points deduction could be imposed by the League for other regulatory matters. Oh to be in the Premiership – or an Argentinean masquerading in West Ham United colours*

Saturday, January 5

FA Cup third round

Huddersfield Town 2 Birmingham City 1

Galpharm Stadium

*Romantics ponder the prospect of a sizeable
upset in the old competition.*

ON a weekend when the smile returned to the FA Cup,
nowhere was it broader than at Huddersfield Town.

A winning goal, finished by a former part-time assistant in
a clothes shop, ensured the tradition of the romantic
underdog prevailing was observed in West Yorkshire. There
was even a role reversal that may yet elevate a famous
victory to folklore status.

Perhaps Birmingham City manager Alex McLeish, in
charge of his first English cup tie, was not entirely *au fait*
with the modern trends of the old competition south of
the border. Thus the Scot selected a side at full strength,
leaving the home team to reshuffle after the Premier
League fashion, hindered as they were by niggling
injuries.

Luke Beckett, who scored the first, and Chris Brandon,
whose left-foot volley nine minutes from time secured a
passage to the fourth round, might not have started on
another afternoon.

"So that was Huddersfield Seconds two, Birmingham First
XI one," chirped one Terriers fan at the final whistle.

Euphoric exaggeration maybe, but for Brandon, this ranks as one of his finest days as a late starter in the professional game.

A left-sided midfielder with non-leaguers Bradford Park Avenue, years of working with dummies in a clothing store clearly smoothed his progress against hapless full backs Stephen Kelly and the chocolate teapot that was Frank Queudrue. For weeks his manager Andy Ritchie has been urging him to arrive late at the far post, and when he did so in the 81st minute, Beckett's marvellously retrieved centre allowed him his moment.

"I played against Chelsea [Huddersfield lost 2-1] a couple of years ago, but this is right up there with the best," said Brandon, 31, who signed professional for Torquay in 1999. "After all, this is the best cup competition in the world."

"Even after they had equalised, we showed a great belief. We have just got to build on this. League One is very tight and we are just a few wins off the play-offs," said Ritchie, who as an instinctive forward was synonymous with Oldham Athletic's renaissance in the late 1980s, was delighted by his former club's success at Everton that marginally eclipsed Huddersfield's feat.

The league, as always, remains the bigger picture, but the manager who lost semi- finals with Oldham and Leeds United as a player does not recoil at the prospect of a lucrative cup run.

"We want another big fish, it's another big pay day for us. Realistically we are not going to win the Cup, but this was fantastic for us, the fans and the town."

Only when the outstanding Fabrice Muamba was on the ball did Birmingham pose menace. His surging run created Gary O'Connor's tap-in leveller after Maik Taylor had fumbled Danny Schofield's tame shot to present Beckett with the early opener.

Confirmation of the gulf in celebrity, if not class, on the day came when Huddersfield captain Andy Holdsworth grabbed a Birmingham shirt at full-time. For Joe Skarz, the 18-year-old substitute left back, there was the consolation of City captain Liam Ridgewell's red No.6 jersey.

Initially, he had asked for Daniel de Ridder's shirt but, apparently, the Dutch winger declined, saying his sister was at the game. If only the Dutchman had stayed in the stands and let his sister wear the shirt from kick-off...

Huddersfield Town (4-5-1): Glennon; Collins, Sinclair, Mirfin, Williams (Skarz 46); Kamara (Jevons 79), Berrett, Holdsworth, Schofield, Brandon; Beckett.
Subs: Smithies (g), Young, Killock.
Booked: Brandon, Skarz, Berrett.

Birmingham City (4-4-2): Taylor; Kely, Jaidi, Ridgewell, Queudrue; McSheffrey, Larsson, Muamba, De Ridder; O'Connor, Forssell (Jerome 62).
Subs: Sadler, Doyle (g), Parnaby, Mutch.
Booked: Queudrue, Ridgewell, Jaidi.

Referee: S Tanner (Somerset).

POSTSCRIPT: *Only the FA Cup could pit Huddersfield away to Oldham in the next round and then a return to Stamford Bridge where once again the trail ended, in the fifth round. Things went from bad to worse for the Bluenoses. Raids by the fraud squad embarrassed officials, but the only real fraud was the team masquerading as a Premier League side. Ultimately found wanting and guilty...and relegated.*

Doncaster Rovers 1 Carlisle United 0

Keepmoat Stadium

A year after uprooting to the Keepmoat Stadium, Doncaster seek to further ambitions and shift up a division to match their environs against one of their closest rivals.

THE four-legged friends, or foes depending on your wager, who compete in Turf racing's oldest Classic are renowned for their stamina and staying power. Fitting then that they run the St Leger in September at Doncaster, where only the hardiest of punters attend having remained loyal through the betting vagaries of a summer's Flat season.

Just across the road from the Town Moor course, Doncaster Rovers once plied their trade against all odds that included a chairman with arson on his mind.

A timely reminder of the Rovers' resilience, though, came with this tenacious 1-0 victory over Carlisle United, a first anniversary celebration of their transfer from Belle Vue to the Keepmoat Stadium.

Just over twelve months on from that move, and half a century since they were relegated from the old Second Division (to tumble into the league basement the following season), Rovers appear on the brink of restoring that status after securing a fourth win in five League One games.

Regaining that rung in the second tier is the burning ambition of chairman John Ryan, although his is a different sort of burning ambition from one of the previous incumbents, Ken Richardson.

Not content with a conviction for conspiracy to defraud and a substantial ban from horse racing after being involved in a duplicitous scam surrounding a nag called Flockton Grey in the 1980s, Richardson moved up a notch or three in the criminal world when he attempted to burn down Belle Vue to claim insurance money in the summer of 1995. A SAS soldier hired to torch the stadium obligingly left his mobile phone in the wooden stand and Richardson was jailed for four years for conspiracy to commit arson.

A decade on, the bulldozers finished the job for him - legally.

Ryan, like many fans, lamented its passing, having once watched Rovers as a young schoolboy from the rickety old terraces.

In an era when football club owners fawn over players like demigods and believe loyalty is valued in points or air miles collected on a credit card, he lends a refreshing air of integrity around south Yorkshire.

When his manager Sean O'Driscoll suffered indifferent results, Ryan stayed calm, and did not take to wearing replica shirts and standing among disgruntled fans disguised cringingly as a 'fake man of the people'.

Instead, as Tammy Wynette advised, he stood by his man, even if the man in question should be forced to hold a megaphone as standard issue for his press conferences. In comparison, Steve Coppell sounds like a garrulous loud-mouth next to the Irishman.

The Keepmoat's largest crowd of the season, 8,197, saw O'Driscoll's team do his talking, very persuasive and eloquent too, laced as it was with a pleasing passing game, even if the scrambled late winner that bounced off substitute James Hayter's knee scarcely did Rovers' superiority justice.

Seconds later, Leeds manager Dennis Wise departed the ground, doubtless impressed by Doncaster's creative tactics that should entertain neutrals at Elland Road when the pair meet this Saturday.

Wise is a pale comparison indeed to Billy Bremner, the equally diminutive but rugged Scotland captain who bossed Leeds with an iron rule from midfield and later took charge at Doncaster where, as a Peterborough United full back, I listened along with colleagues as his squeaky Scottish tones tore strips of paint off the adjacent home team dressing room wall after inflicting a thoroughly undeserved 4-0 defeat on the home team.

It remains one of the very best managerial impersonations of spontaneous combustion, ranking alongside Martin O'Neill's every Saturday afternoon during his Leicester City stewardship.

Wise was roundly jeered as he left his seat. How Rovers' fans are relishing the north west passage across their county at the weekend.

Seven years ago, Leeds were European Cup semi-finalists and finished fourth in the Premiership. A few days before Leeds lost in Valencia, Rovers were beaten 2-1 by Telford United, ending their third season in the Conference perched ninth behind Southport and Leigh RMI.

Fortunately, the 2,026 fans at Belle Vue that day, Ryan among them, understood that they were there for the long-haul. Stamina, loyalty and a refusal to pander to populist notion. Concepts seemingly lost on Leeds' Peter Ridsdale; eternally enshrined amid the Rovers return.

Doncaster Rovers (4-3-3): Sullivan; O'Connor, S Roberts, Lockwood, G Roberts; Green, Stock (Wilson 83), Wellens; Coppinger (Hayter 80), McCammon (Guy 80), Price.
Subs: Woods, McDaid.
Booked: Wellens.
Goal: Hayter (84) .

Carlisle United (4-4-2): Westwood; Raven (Gall 90), Livesey, Murphy, Aranalde; Smith, Lumsdon, Bridge-Wilkinson, Hackney (Carlton 75); Graham, Garner.
Subs: Howarth (g), Gall, Joyce, Arnison.
Booked: Garner, Carlton, Aranalde, Bridge-Wilkinson.

Referee: L Mason (Lancashire).

POSTSCRIPT: *Doncaster duly went to Leeds and savoured a historic 1-0 victory over their 'posher' county rivals. It got better, too.*

"I first came here as a boy in 1958, the year we were relegated from the old Second Division," recalled John Ryan. "Obviously I blame myself! So when I took over here, I was determined to put it right and restore us to Championship level."

Ryan's enigmatic presence is nothing short of remarkable, given that the local schoolboy's first game witnessed a 6-1 home defeat by Fulham. Jimmy Hill scored five for the visitors.

That was something of a nadir for the young Ryan – as well as being born too late to see the likes of Peter Doherty, the gifted Northern Ireland inside forward, orchestrate a Rovers side of '50s vintage acknowledged as their finest.

It included Charlie Williams, a solid centre-half and later comedian whose catchline extended 'flower' power into the 1970s, and Alick Jeffrey, acclaimed as the finest of all Rovers players. The equivalent of Wayne Rooney in drainpipe trousers,

Jeffrey was destined to sign for Matt Busby's Babes at Manchester United before a double fracture of his leg playing for England Under-23s interrupted his career and ambitions.

Hard to make a case for any of the current players being able even to lace Jeffrey's boots, but Ryan's express wish of regaining the second tier status he saw as a schoolboy was realised when Rovers won their play-off final at Wembley 1-0. Against Leeds United. Who else?

Saturday, January 19

Swindon Town 2 Nottingham Forest 1

County Ground

*New owners bring the inevitable brave new world and dawn
to a saturated Wiltshire where Swindon are striving,
somewhat optimistically, for the play-offs.*

TIME was when red revolutionaries favoured the figure five
in triumphing their claims for a better future.

At Swindon Town, though, they do not believe in doing
things by half and thus a ten-point plan was unveiled in the
match day programme on Saturday as a new consortium
revealed its strategy to revive fortunes at the County Ground.

Inflation and a generation prone to New Labour, Big
Brother and exaggeration may have played its part, but it
seems that, given a lack of Gulag development in Wiltshire
and without recourse to exile dissidents to the frozen wastes
of Abersoch or Anglesey, the current Swindon board stand a
far better chance of fulfilling their promises than dear old
Joseph Stalin ever did.

Confirmation that they mean business was delivered by
Maurice Malpas, the man they selected as manager. A
surprise appointment given the usual suspects in contention
for the job, the Scot enjoyed a rousing victory after his first
game in charge as promotion-chasing Nottingham Forest
were beaten 2-1 in the mud and sludge.

With games in hand, Malpas remains optimistic that a
League One play-off position can be secured. An FA Cup

replay at Barnet tomorrow night may reap further rewards.

Certainly anything is possible if opponents are as generous as Forest, who scored all three goals but deservedly departed defeated.

James Perch nodded Swindon ahead from Jon Paul McGovern's free kick, and it was not until Nathan Tyson's searing pace was unleashed from the bench that Forest posed menace. Luke Chambers levelled from a corner yet it was another McGovern centre that provided the winner as Ian Breckin headed beyond his own goalkeeper eight minutes from time.

Chairman Andrew Fitton was celebrating with a glass of vin rouge in the corridors later. Small wonder. Since his arrival, a transfer embargo has been lifted and the side is unbeaten. Even the previous chairman Sir Seton Wills, whose family have owned the club since the troubled days of demotion due to financial irregularities in the early 1990s, was lavish in his praise.

"They are the best people to take it forward," he said, referring to them as the 'Ramsbury Mafia', reference to a nearby town where three members of the board have roots.

In fact, the wealthy triumvirate of Fitton, Sir Martyn Arbib and Jeremy Wray now reside from London to Barbados but their affinity with the local community is a pleasing rarity in an era when Dubai-based concerns and American dollars are infiltrating Europe's city of culture and England's second city landscape.

Twenty years ago Fitton, who admits to being 'passionate' about his football, was offered his hometown club Newcastle United for £3m. Some years later, a trusted friend told him he would have him 'certified' if he ever invested in a football club.

Still legally sane, Fitton has not rested on his laurels. Not satisfied with one club, he is chairman of two. The FA have given him permission to retain his links with Hungerford Town, where on Saturday morning he gave a pep talk before the Hellenic Premier club reached the last 16 of the FA Vase, in tandem with Swindon until the end of the season.

"There's the old story of businessmen leaving their brains at the door when they go into a football club," Fitton said. "You have to guard against that."

Memo to board. Check contents of grey matter upon leaving County Ground. Amendment to blueprint in new-improved, bigger better 11 point plan.

Swindon Town (4-4-2): Brezovan; Comminges, Ifil, Aljofree, Vincent; McGovern, Peacock, Easton, Zaaboub; Paynter, Sturrock (Ashikodi 78).
Subs: Roberts, Nicholas, Pook, McNamee.
Booked: Comminges, Ashikodi.
Goals: Perch (35 og), Breckin (82 og).

Notttingham Forest (4-4-2): Smith; Chambers, Breckin, Morgan, Lockwood (Wilson 82); Davies, McGugan, Cohen, Perch; Holt, Commons (Tyson 53).
Subs: Roberts (g), Lennon, Bennett.
Booked: Holt, Bennett, Tyson.
Goal: Chambers (63).

Referee: M Thorpe (Suffolk).

POSTSCRIPT: *Swindon could not sustain that level of commitment nor endeavour and eventually the rather ambitious hopes of the play-offs drifted serenely away. "We have a philosophy in everything we do, a Japanese philosophy of continuous improvement," the engaging chairman Andrew Fitton had said when taking over. "A journey of a million miles*

starts with one small step. If you speak to a Japanese factory worker their aim in life is to improve by one per cent a month. Over five years it is a 120 per cent improvement."
Unfortunately, our manufacturing industry all but vanished years ago, decimated by strikes, unabated foreign competition and the inexorable rise of paper-clip counters. Patience was observed on the British Leyland shop floor as much as it is on the Old Trafford terraces...i.e. rarely if ever. Maybe Swindon fans embrace patience as a virtue and will grant Fitton's strategy, that most valuable of football assets to succeed...time will tell.

Saturday, February 2

Leeds United 0 Tranmere Rovers 2

Elland Road

A faltering Leeds side look to an old favourite to restore confidence, pride and ultimately status. So no pressure then...

DURING his playing stylish career, Gary McAllister once turned up for a job interview with Brian Clough sporting cowboy boots, prompting the Nottingham Forest manager to quiz the Scotland midfielder about his sexual orientation.

The boots have long gone, along with the hair, but McAllister's return to Elland Road on Saturday managed to evoke the best cowboy traditions with a sting in the tale to equal *Brokeback Mountain*.

With the departure of that pesky mini-cab scrapper and saloon bar gunslinger Johnny Ringo, aka Dennis 'Wisey' Wise, Leeds United owner and former dairy cattle baron Ken Bates appointed McAllister as his replacement after discussions in Monaco last Tuesday.

His brief was simple. Steady an ailing team, spruce up their act from long-ball brawlers to passing purists and win promotion from League One. And, by the way, you have four months, the term of your contract, to succeed.

In the more civilised Wild West of Yorkshire, where the mean streets are largely safe to walk since Ian Bowyer was kicked out of town, this remains a tough mission – even for Randolph Scott and a ten-gallon Stetson.

McAllister, an elegant, perceptive performer who lifted the First Division title with Leeds in 1992, still embraces those virtues as a manager. Yet if he is the antithesis of his predecessor, the size of this task soon became apparent as Tranmere Rovers triumphed 2-0 at a soulless Elland Road, a fourth straight victory that hoisted them into the last play-off place held previously by Leeds.

"I'm not here for the money," declared McAllister with the conviction of a man who wants to restore fortunes in the long-term. Certainly, if his arrival was meant to encourage the populist vote, the ploy has worked despite a certain apathy reflected in a mediocre attendance.

Yet even in the *Land of Make Believe* that Leeds frequent occasionally in the form of the match day programme league table that refuses to acknowledge the club's 15-points deduction, Leeds are no longer top.

In the real world, they are now eighth as initially a rare moment of quality from on-loan Bristol City winger Jennison Myrie-Williams signalled a deserved lead for the visitors. Ian Moore, known to his manager Ronnie as "son", headed another to mark his second debut for Tranmere, back at one of his many former employees.

The side in Don Revie-fashioned white had floundered; the men in black had won.

A reversal of the natural order in screen western terms.

Although with Leeds on centre stage, even with McAllister at the helm, sorting the good guys from the bad is seldom straightforward.

Leeds United (4-4-2): Lucas; Kenton (Carole 53), Michalik, Heath, Sheehan (Huntington 74); Prutton, Howson, Hughes, Johnson; Elding (Flo 57), Beckford
Subs: Martin (g), Sweeney.
Booked: none.

Tranmere Rovers (4-4-2): Coyne; Stockdale, Kay, Goodison, Taylor; Williams (Curran 90), Jennings, McLaren, Sherriff; Zola (Greenacre 85), Moore.
Subs: Mullin, Chorley, Achterberg (g).
Booked: Zola.
Goals: Williams (61), Moore (69).

Referee: S Mathieson (Cheshire).

POSTSCRIPT: *McAllister fulfilled his part of the bargain in reviving the struggling Leeds Dennis Wise had left behind. But while he delivered a place in the play-off final, his players were unable to land a knockout blow, not even a telling one in fact, on Doncaster Rovers at Wembley. McAllister remains in charge, determined to secure the automatic promotion denied them by the 15-points penalty deduction. Tranmere's cause was never so strong again, the Wirral club fading from the promotion equation to finish a disappointing, in the context of earlier promise, tenth.*

Saturday, February 9

Lincoln City 2 Rochdale 1

Sincil Bank

During the week when some Premier League bigwigs were advocating 'the 39 steps' plan to play abroad, Lincoln's home comforts were required to sustain a revival against the form team more than happy to travel.

THE running joke was that Keith Alexander had won part of the previous night's EuroMillions lottery. Certainly the BBC Radio Lincolnshire pundit for this League Two game at Sincil Bank knows a thing or two about numbers.

Specifically when his was almost up as manager of Lincoln City. Close to death after suffering a cerebral aneurysm in November 2003, only the surgical skills of medical staff saved him.

Four successive play-off failures with Lincoln, then sacked by Peterborough United after procuring the non-league forward pair that is currently inspiring Posh's promotion push, and an acrimonious departure from Bury, suggest that Lady Luck has not been so kind in the ensuing years.

"I'm lucky to be alive, really," he countered. A cordial chap, he doesn't bang on about how he was England's first black manager (which he was before Keith Curle then Paul Ince swelled the ranks) or blabber on about racial inequality, preferring instead to let his team's results demonstrate his ability rather than the colour of his skin.

Peter Jackson directs traffic in the Churchillian fashion from the dugout. The Lincoln manager was forced to stand down from his job because of illness, but not before he had revived the Imps' fortunes and secured the manager of the month award for February.

Pic courtesy of Lincoln City FC: Andrew Vaughan

He was talking in between summarising duties that included praise for his former club's dogged 2-1 victory over Rochdale, a third consecutive win that has lifted spirits and the team that added a fifth play-off debacle last season to Alexander's quartet.

Rather like some of our less honourable members of Parliament and Cabinet ministers, Rochdale are happy to play away from home.

Unbeaten on their travels since the opening day, when they were thrashed 3-0 by Peterborough United, Rochdale's own play-off aspirations seemed rosy when Rene Howe atoned for earlier profligacy by levelling Jamie Forrester's goal in first-half stoppage time after goalkeeper Sam Russell obligingly dropped Lee Frecklington's free kick at his feet.

As the visitors dictated, though, Daniel Hone stuck out a right boot and prodded the winner with nine minutes remaining. With games in hand, Rochdale still have the chance to stake a claim to automatic promotion, but manager Keith Hill was far from amused, hinting darkly that his goalkeeper cannot keep making silly mistakes. Jobs on the line, changes afoot, even a yard, sort of talk.

What the myopic critics of those Premier League philanthropists attempting to arrest our declining export industry have failed to see is that by shipping the odd game or three abroad, there will at long last be someone, somewhere, even in a Chelsea shirt, who could actually claim to be an indigenous talent rather than the imported Foreign Legion that blight or brighten our national game, depending on your point of view and club's bank balance, of course.

Local hero Daniel Hone is about to pounce for the winner that jolted Rochdale's play-off surge temporarily. His subsequent celebration was not quite so impressive.

Pic courtesy of Lincoln City FC: Andrew Vaughan

In the humbler environs of the cathedral city, Lincoln folk can settle on Hone as their local hero as the 18-year-old secured his first league goal and a bottle of champagne for a man-of-the-match performance.

A centre of media attention later, his composure was briefly rattled when an apprentice colleague 'mooned' during his live radio interview, confirmation that some football traditions, whilst constant, are best kept at home.

While Jackson effused about his teenage defender, he lamented the loss of coach Neil McDonald to Leeds earlier that week. Would Terry Yorath be his replacement? "I'm still talking to Jurgen Klinsmann," Jackson joked. At least the German might tutor young Hone in the art of goal celebration. Jackson described his first effort as 'the worst I have ever seen'.

Three points in the bag and Lincoln edging gradually away from relegation, the post-match music was apposite. *'Always look on the bright side of life…'*

Up in the stands, the Life of Keith, so precious over the past five years, would concur.

Lincoln City (4-4-2): Marriott; Brown, Hone, Beevers, Ridley; N'Guessan (Ryan 86), Frecklington, Kerr, Dodds; Stallard (Wright 79), Forrester.
Subs: Moses, Hand, Duffy (g).
Booked: Dodds.
Goals: Forrester (45), Hone (81).

Rochdale (4-4-2): Russell; Ramsden, Stanton, McArdle (Holness 21), Kennedy; Perkins, Doolan, Jones, Rundle (Thorpe 82); Howe, Le Fondre (Higginbotham 71)
Subs: Basham, Spencer (g).
Booked: Higginbotham, Stanton.
Goal: Howe (56).

Referee: A Woolmer (Northamptonshire).

POSTSCRIPT: *By poignant quirk of fate, Peter Jackson found himself a victim of serious illness when he was diagnosed with throat cancer later that week. He eventually stepped down from his post to receive treatment, but not before two more wins, thus compiling a sequence of five consecutive victories, earning him the divisional manager of the month award for February. He was presented with his prize before his last game in charge, a 1-0 win over Wycombe Wanderers on March 1, driving away from the ground determined to return in the summer.*

In contrast, Rochdale lost four of their five February games, predictably winning away at Bradford City. They recovered to claim a play-off place, but after beating Darlington on penalties in the semi finals, Stockport County triumphed 3-2 at Wembley to deny them what could have been only a second promotion in the club's history as it celebrated its centenary season. For Keith Alexander, February proved a more productive month when he was appointed manager of ailing Macclesfield. Few thought the Silkmen would survive another season in the Football League, but an impressive sequence of results steered them safely clear of the relegation places and ensured a happy ending to the season for Alexander.

Nottingham Forest 1 Swindon Town 0

City Ground

Forest have the chance to reverse recent fortunes and of swift vengeance after losing at the County Ground a month ago.

AN impressive 'Eye' has hoisted revolution to new heights in Nottingham's Old Market Square as a newly-erected giant carousel confronts the civic corridors of power in the adjacent Council House.

On a clear day, passengers can oversee the less salubrious areas of Hyson Green and St Ann's that have been stigmatised in a city somewhat harshly renowned as the gun capital of Great Britain.

For Colin Calderwood the feeling of unjust scrutiny has also been intense in recent weeks.

In many ways, the Nottingham Forest manager would wish that he could become as anonymous as 'one of those little dots' of people that a pitiless Harry Lime referred to spinning high above the ground in post-war Vienna.

Instead, Calderwood has been enduring a fraught football version of Russian roulette as he sends out a side never knowing whether the chamber is fully loaded or firing blanks in the struggle to clinch automatic promotion from League One.

Although the natives have been growing restless, there are some quarters of the City Ground who believe it is those in higher office who should grasp a loaded service revolver and retire to the study to do the decent thing for the shambles to

Nathan Tyson celebrates the only goal of the game that avenged an earlier defeat by Swindon. In frustratingly familiar fashion, the forward then limped off with a recurrence of a hamstring strain.

Pic courtesy of the Nottingham Evening Post

which the former European Cup winners have been reduced.

At least the last week has provided respite, culminating in a solid if uninspiring 1-0 victory over Swindon Town that followed an improved performance to take a point at Leeds United on Tuesday night.

Since Doncaster carelessly left their Keepmoat pitch open to the elements, allowing Jack Frost to postpone their game with Leeds United, the victory lifted Forest to within three points of second-placed Rovers, who they play away in what is certain to be a frantic finale to the season.

Kris Commons relies on his trusty left foot to open up the Swindon rearguard. Nicknamed 'puff' by his team mates, perhaps a touch of the magic dragon and certainly an inspiration to Forest on many occasions. His close season move to bitter local rivals Derby County may incite other sobriquets from the Trent End.

Pic courtesy of the Nottingham Evening Post

Before that, more promotion rivals in Carlisle United (tomorrow night) and Leyton Orient this weekend must be visited. If it is a few days that shape Forest's destiny and Calderwood's future at the club they will be suffered without the influential Nathan Tyson, whose exceptional pace and predatory sense secured the 50th minute winner against a sluggish Swindon.

Tyson retired shortly after with a recurring hamstring tweak that precludes him for at least a couple of games. Relying on his forward partner Junior Agogo may not cure Calderwood's unease. The Ghana forward returned in fanfare and with a swagger in his ungainly gait from the African Cup of Nations with Portsmouth reportedly offering £2.5million for the player, although as one terrace wag suggested, he would have driven him to the South Coast himself if the offer had been serious.

When the player fluffed an open goal, created by Tyson's centre, it was suddenly very easy to understand the thinking behind the mercy dash to Fratton Park.

With Swansea City almost out of sight at the top, the chasing pack are, in effect, vying for one automatic place, a mirror of last season when Scunthorpe charged clear leaving Bristol City to clinch second and Forest to fail alarmingly in the play-offs.

What goes round, comes round may be Calderwood's hope. As long as he's not stranded on the bottom of the carousel when the ride grinds to a shuddering halt.

Nottingham Forest (4-3-3): Smith; Chambers, Morgan, Wilson, Lockwood; Clingan, McGugan (Perch 87), Cohen; Tyson (Davies 74), Agogo (Sinclair 85), Commons.
Subs: Breckin, Richardson (g).
Booked: Morgan, Chambers, Perch.
Goal: Tyson (50).

Swindon Town (4-4-2): Brezovan; Comminges, Ifil, Aljofree, Vincent; McGovern (Zaaboub 84), Pook, Easton, McNamee (Roberts 60); Paynter, Sturrock (Ashikodi 71)
Subs: Smith (g), Kanyuka.
Booked: Ifil.

Referee: D Foster (Tyne and Wear).

An anxious Colin Calderwood watches his Forest charges struggle
to an unconvincing victory over one his former clubs.

Pic courtesy of the Nottingham Evening Post

Saturday, February 23

Bournemouth 2 Cheltenham Town 2

Dean Court

*The home team, short in points and their pay packet, need a
win against one of their relegation rivals as administration
and its subsequent penalties begin to bite hard.*

THE relentless grunting of political snouts in slimy troughs
was echoing around Bournemouth last Thursday. A
familiarity that breeds voters' contempt like no other, news
that councillors had been awarded pay rises of 36 per-cent
was greeted with dismay by residents accusing Town Hall
officials of jumping on the gravy train.

But just when weary cynicism seemed to be eroding
further the faith in human nature on the South Coast, a
glimmer of restoration emerged at the local football club.

Following a meeting with the PFA at Dean Court on the
same day, Bournemouth players agreed to defer half of their
wages – that's a 50 per-cent pay cut councillor – until further
notice as the troubled League One club sinks or swims in the
mire of administration.

"We are doing it for the club because if we don't, there isn't
going to be a club any more," said Josh Gowling, the team's PFA
representative, who added the decision had been unanimous.

The caring, sharing ethos appeared to be infectious on
Saturday as Bournemouth relinquished a two-goal cushion
and allowed relegation rivals Cheltenham Town to escape
with a valuable point and remain outside the bottom four.

Despite the programme platitudes of bellicose resistance by chairman, manager and club captain Darren Anderton (absent, injured - it almost goes without printing), the ten-point penalty is almost certain to relegate Bournemouth, who played spiritedly after Max-Alain Gradel's penalty and a clever lob from Marvin Bartley established a 2-0 lead before David Bird pegged one back shortly before the interval.

Yet, so incensed was the normally placid Cheltenham manager Keith Downing with his team that the former Notts County midfielder hit the hair-dryer button on turbo and sent his team back out onto the pitch during half-time, a sort of public humiliation without the stocks and rotten fruit on sale. Shame, really.

Suitably chastened, Cheltenham rallied and were rewarded by Steve Brooker's late leveller from an Alan Wright corner, two veteran baldies rejoicing like Bros reunited on tour. Scott Brown's red card for a lunge on the equally culpable Bartley was an undeserving finale for the visitors.

The current Dean Court, of course, is not the ground where Ted MacDougall smacked nine past Southern League part-timers Margate in the FA Cup under the leadership of the flamboyant John Bond, nor indeed where George Best made his final bow in League football, attracted by then manager Don Megson and the prospect of sun, sand and sea - the sangria and sex he reserved for London excursions apparently.

Such heritage is entitled to a degree of preservation, although some unabated Cherries picking, the ground is owned and leased by a London property group, is a hindrance to potential buyers with former manager Harry Redknapp reported to be willing to help financially if a suitable consortium was assembled.

Above: Josh Gowling, who moved to Carlisle United
in the summer, gets a foot in ahead of Steve Brooker,
Cheltenham's saviour with a late equaliser.

Pics courtesy of Michael Cunningham

Below: Max-Alain Gradel, having opened the scoring
from the penalty spot, gets to grips with David Bird.

Marvin Bradley is hugged by Josh Gowling after securing a two-goal lead for Bournemouth. Jason Pearce (with head bandage) stands by awaiting his turn.

Pic courtesy of Michael Cunningham.

Bond's son, Kevin, is now at the Bournemouth helm, a little too calm in choppy waters for his own good. Shaken or stirred might be better. In the meantime, young Gowling expresses the wider concerns.

"It's a tough time for all of us, we've all got mortgages to pay and the married lads have kids to look after," the 24-year-old defender said.

Armed with those powers of persuasion over co-workers, perhaps a career in politics beckons. An acceptable face as opposed to New Labour and New Dave? Who knows? Certainly, his earlier career path in the notoriously fickle Black Country with West Bromwich Albion, then a sabbatical differentiating between his smörgåsbord and his tactics board, is certain to have enhanced his credentials as an ambassador at home and abroad.

However, a genuine smile and a willingness to accept salary reductions and responsibility, allied to inexperience in the field of kissing babies' heads, may prove his downfall.

Bournemouth (4-4-2): Stewart; Young, Gowling, Pearce, Cummings; Gradel, Bartley, Cooper, Bradbury; Vokes (Pitman 86), Kuffour (Tessem78).
Subs: Pryce (g), McQuiod, Partington.
Booked: Cummings, Gradel.
Goals: Gradel (pen) (16); Bartley (39).

Cheltenham Town (4-4-2): Higgs; Gill, Gallinagh, Duff, Wright; D'Agostino (Vincent 46), Bird, Armstrong, (Connor 78), Lindegaard (S Brown 46); Brooker, Gillespie.
Subs: Spencer. S P Brown (g).
Booked: Vincent.
Sent off: S Brown.
Goals: Bird (45), Brooker (88).

Referee: D Drysdale (Lincolnshire).

Saturday, March 1

Wrexham 1 Mansfield Town 1

Racecourse Ground

As the stragglers oppose each other in League Two, the bottom two collide in North Wales in the hope of improving their prospects of escaping demotion.

OOP North, as those upwardly mobile southern Yuppies might have mimicked, they often gravitated to life in the lower strata. In Wales and Nottinghamshire, that tradition of heading down to earn a crust, occasionally a fatal attraction to colliers in Wrexham and Mansfield, is being observed manfully by the football teams of those former pit communities.

Once borne out of financial expediency, the attraction is now more macabre, inexplicable, one of the Racecourse Ground's largest crowds of the season drawn to this humiliating League Two relegation slugfest like Victorian spectators to the gallows for a public hanging or Terry Wogan to Eurovision.

Michael Boulding, the Mansfield forward whose 20th goal of the season secured a merited lead, recently finished a review of *Forsaken, Afghan Women* by Lana Slezic for his local newspaper. Completing that thankless task must have been akin to reading a Thomas the Tank Engine picture storybook compared to wading through this desperate saga.

Not that either manager needed to apologise for the state of play. Yet with all four bottom sides in opposition at the weekend, a 1-1 draw here and at Macclesfield, who drew with Notts County, failed to assuage fears for Football League survival.

On St David's Day, and sporting commemorative red shirts, Wrexham were unable to force the win, even after Michael Proctor's 70th minute free kick that breached the defensive wall had raised expectations.

"It could be vital at the end of the season," said Proctor, who talked about the 'massive' local derby at Chester this weekend. It was the reverse fixture last November that saw Brian Little's return to football, first taking charge of a game at the Racecourse on his 54th birthday.

Despite a decent point then, Wrexham lingered, as now, rooted at the foot of the table. The feeling is they will remain there, languishing adrift of safety without the prospect of clinging to a last-match inflatable that victory over Boston United provided last May.

With games in hand on their rivals and all of them to play, Mansfield's salvation is within reach, however. While defeat for Wrexham would have virtually condemned them to the lower level, it would have been a seventh consecutive away win for the visitors without Proctor's intervention, which he described as 'getting out of jail'.

A decent analogy for Alcatraz or Stalag Luft III perhaps given that his free-kick squeezed through the narrowest of gaps and was executed as a result of meticulous planning. Clearly, though, the former Sunderland forward who once scored goals in the Premiership has not been banged up inside one of HM's open prisons lately.

"We will have days like this but we need to stick together," said Mansfield's battle-worn manager Billy Dearden, veteran survivor of relegation dogfights both with Mansfield and Notts County previously.

Dearden's side may require more of the good fortune that brought the opener, a Keith Briggs shot steered into the net by Boulding, something that would have been anathema in his teenage years as a tennis prodigy who shared rooms with Tim Henman on the ATP tour.

Off the pitch, though, a torturous takeover from owner Keith Haslam, reviled by most Mansfield fans, seems to have endured longer than Bruce Forsyth's stage career.

It was in 1977 that these two sides staged a dramatic finale at the Racecourse where 22,000 witnessed an Ernie Moss effort snatch promotion to the old Second Division from Wrexham, the first and last time Mansfield ascended to such heady heights.

Of course Liverpool and Kevin Keegan were winning with irritating regularity back then. It was that long ago.

The current crop departed to deafening silence on Saturday, a muteness inspired by apathy and anxiety perhaps. *The Boys from the Blackstuff* are sinking fast. The demonic Yozzer Hughes pleading 'Giz a job' springs worryingly to mind.

Wrexham (3-4-3): Ward; Bolland, Hope,
M Williams (Aiston 61); Spender, Whitley, Spann, Tremarco;
Broughton (Duffy 71), Proctor, Llewellyn (Hall 61)
Subs: A Williams (g), Nicholson.
Booked: Bolland.
Goal: Proctor (70).

Mansfield Town (4-4-2): Muggleton; Wood, Mullins,
Buxton, Jellyman; Hamshaw (Arnold 46), Briggs,
D'Laryea, Atkinson; Louis, Boulding.
Subs: White (g), Brown, Martin, Holmes.
Booked: none.
Goal: Boulding (53).

Referee: P Taylor (Hertfordshire).

POSTSCRIPT: *Billy Dearden's own survival prospects in a managerial capacity diminished rapidly with a 4-0 home defeat by Rochdale the following week, and the old war horse was gone before Hereford United arrived to inflict a fortuitous 1-0 defeat on the Tuesday night. Despite the shuffling of personnel, there were to be no dramatic changes at the foot of the table.*

Monday, March 3

Nottingham Forest 0 Carlisle United 1

City Ground

*The live television cameras visit Forest for
an appetising top-of-the-table showdown.*

THE burden of expectation has long been a companion of
Nottingham Forest, rather like an unwanted house guest
outstaying their welcome.

Its presence emerged once more at the City Ground last
night as Carlisle United secured a precious victory and thus
seized the initiative in the chase to join runaway League One
leaders Swansea City in the Championship next season.

Danny Graham's 13th goal of the season was enough to
claim the win and second position in the table, moving two
points clear of Doncaster Rovers.

It is not the first time Forest have suffered stage fright
when Sky and a capacity crowd camp out on the south
bank of the Trent. The home side had their chances,
mostly inspired by Kris Commons, who was denied by
Kieren Westwood on a number of occasions, most notably
when the Carlisle goalkeeper pushed away the Forest
player's free kick late on. However, Westwood's finest
moment came midway through the first half when he
thwarted Julian Bennett's firm header with an athletic tip
over the crossbar.

Carlisle, though, could claim a penalty was denied them
when Grant Holt hauled down Evan Horwood with a leading

arm, an obvious foul missed by the referee but not the television cameras.

Marc Bridge-Wilkinson also squandered the best opening of the match when he somehow failed to connect with David Raven's centre in the 50th minute and Grant Smith was also profligate when the Carlisle full back played creator once more, Smith failing to hit the target when his colleague found him in space inside the penalty area with a clever run and pass.

In front of Forest's best attendance this season, Graham saw that a certain justice was seen to be done when Paul Smith fumbled a routine take in the Forest goal and the Carlisle forward pounced with an assured finish from a tight angle to score his fourth goal in the last six games.

Nottingham Forest (4-3-3): Smith;
Perch (McCleary 87), Morgan, Wilson, Bennett;
McGugan (Davies 75), Clingan, Cohen;
Commons, Agogo Holt.
Subs: Lockwood, Thornhill, Richardson (g).

Carlisle United (4-5-1): Westwood; Raven, Livesey,
Murphy, Horwood; Taylor, Bridge-Wilkinson,
G Smith (J Smith74), Lumsdon, Hackney (Carlton 84);
Graham (Madine 90).
Subs: Howarth (g), Carlton, Arnison, Madine.
Booked: Bridge-Wilkinson.
Goal: Graham (71).

Referee: M Atkinson (West Yorkshire).

POSTSCRIPT: *As the games slipped agonisingly away, Carlisle's return to the second tier of the domestic game after an absence of 22 years seemed increasingly likely, but the Cumbrians hit a brick wall in the crucial stages and were* *reduced to relying on the lottery of the play-offs, where they swiftly discovered the folly of gambling, losing 3-2 to Leeds United on aggregate as Gary McAllister's team stole the advantage, as they had done on so many occasions that season, with a decisive last minute goal in the second leg at Brunton Park.*

Saturday, March 8

Walsall 0 Northampton Town 2

Banks's Stadium

Walsall seek to continue their unlikely but encouraging progress towards a second successive promotion.

THERE'S a lot of the Ernie Wise in Walsall Football Club. Short, fat hairy legs aside – and plenty of those graced the Banks's Stadium at the weekend. The League One club also must settle for second best billing, as did Eric Morecambe's little mate, a diminutive package not dissimilar to the Black Country ground.

While Wise probably was the nation's second favourite comedian behind his partner, Walsall continue to be the Midlands' second favourite football team. And nobody takes them seriously.

It is a bugbear that commercial director Roy Whalley touched upon, insisting that promotion to the Championship might engender a sense of 'civic pride' in the club and inspire crowds towards the 12,000 capacity mark rather than the half full houses that are attracted currently.

With neighbours Wolverhampton Wanderers and West Bromwich Albion not playing, and Aston Villa equally idle on Saturday, a slightly inflated 6,844 turned up for Walsall's first home match in a month.

Sadly, and true to form in these matters, the home side failed to join them and were routed 2-0 by Northampton Town, worthy winners whose own play-off aspirations were revived by two excellent Adebayo Akinfenwa goals, his sixth in as many games since joining the Cobblers from Millwall in January.

Despite securing promotion last May, manager Richard Money endured sporadic booing as the side floundered early in the season, touching a nerve in the former Liverpool player.

The booing, again intermittent and low key, returned as Walsall toiled in a game that Money described as a 'bad day at the office' for his players.

Money appeared to be on the brink of a serious rant during his post-match deliberations but refrained somehow from castigating support, either lacking in numbers or encouragement.

In truth, Walsall's following remained vociferously loyal, even after Akinfenwa's clever lob eluded that most cavalier of custodians Clayton Ince, whose erratic shenanigans might have raised an eyebrow on the bench in Jim Barron and Eric McManus.

Barron enjoyed a distinguished career between the white posts that peeked with Nottingham Forest in the First Division, while McManus enjoyed some memorable moments sporting the green jersey at Notts County and Stoke City among others, before ending up as the respective coaches in the art of goalkeeping at Northampton and Walsall.

Ince was blameless, however, when Akinfenwa headed a second from Danny Jackman's centre, instigating a convoluted three-part goal celebration that praises the Almighty, his wife and young daughter. Small wonder the poor chap was substituted shortly after, doubtless exhausted and worried sick a hat-trick could have tipped him over the edge.

In terms of 'bad days at the office', Tommy Mooney was spilling coffee on the Xerox machine just as the boss was photocopying his posterior for posterity. The Walsall captain fluffed two left-foot volleys he normally finishes in style and a late flourish was destined to failure.

A couple of fine away victories had thrust Walsall into fifth place, where they remain, a position of which Money maintains 'in no way should we be there', reference to rapid progression exceeding expectation.

After Brighton at the old Bescot tomorrow night, Walsall travel to Nottingham Forest then Leeds.

Perhaps then parties on both sides of the fence might begin to appreciate the value of home comforts.

Walsall (4-4-2): Ince; Weston (Dobson 81), Roper, Gerrard, Boertien (Deeney 70); Betsy, Bardley, Wrack, Holmes; Moore (Taundry 62), Mooney.
Subs: Bossi (g), Nicholls.
Booked: Weston.

Northampton Town (3-5-2): Bunn; Little, Hughes, Gyepes; Crowe (Coke 23), Gilligan, Burnell, Jackman, Holt; Henderson (Larkin 86), Akinfenwa (Hubertz 74).
Subs: Dunn (g), Jones.
Booked: Hughes.
Goals: Akinfenwa (8, 71).

Referee: A Haines (Tyne and Wear).

POSTSCRIPT: *Walsall's decline continued at home to Brighton in midweek and their season ended tamely, winning just two of their remaining 11 games. Still, a mid-table finish in 13th position, ultimately three places behind Northampton, was a decent enough reward you might have thought. Even so, Money resigned his post, thus ending an uneasy relationship at Walsall and the Black Country fans with whom he seldom seemed comfortable.*

Saturday, March 15

Peterborough United 0 Notts County 0

London Road

*Posh chairman Darragh MacAnthony anticipates
an avalanche of goals as struggling Notts County
pay a visit to his table-topping side.*

THE post-match talk in the London Road boardroom
revolved around budgets and forward planning as a
considerable chunk of the early Saturday night passed
oblivious to the directors and management team discussing
blueprints for the future.

The longevity and intensity of the meeting reflected
Darragh MacAnthony's infrequent visits to the club he owns.
Shrewd in business and healthy options, the Peterborough
United chairman prefers to 'winter' in Florida where his
overseas property investment company flourishes.

Billboards adorned by his visage, strewn alongside huge
bouvelards, have been known to surprise the unsuspecting
tourist near Kissimmee and Orlando, perhaps a blessing for
the mostly British intake who eventually may tire of being
stalked by grown men and women in mouse costumes by the
middle week of their fortnight in Disney nirvana.

Now the engaging Irishman may consider spending even
more time in the Sunshine State, perhaps to the end of May,
after Peterborough relinquished pole position in League Two
following a 0-0 gridlock against relegation candidates Notts
County at the weekend.

On his previous trip to London Road, in January, MacAnthony saw the Posh lose to Macclesfield since when they embarked upon a 12-game unbeaten sequence in the league, winning 11 of those to overhaul MK Dons at the top of the table.

In fairness, a club record-equalling ninth consecutive win was denied them, more by a marvellously resilient County back four and the safe handling of goalkeeper Russell Hoult rather than the chairman's portentous presence.

Yet there is the chance to allay the superstitious of mind should MacAnthony turn up at stadium:mk on Good Friday, a tricky one of course since new leaders the Dons will fancy their chances of repeating the victory over Peterborough last December that extended their lead at the summit against what were once more their closest rivals.

"We'll be looking forward to that and preparing for it," said Peterborough manager Darren Ferguson. "I've told the lads not to be too disappointed because we didn't resort to humping it to try and break them open.

"They defended well and invited us to try and get behind them, but unfortunately we couldn't do it. By next Friday we could be back on top of the league.

"The main thing is the chairman is committed to trying to tie up our best young players because, as I've said many times before, we want to take this club not just up one division but two at least."

Visiting tickets are sold out and those travelling know that the formidable front pairing of Craig Mackail-Smith and Aaron Mclean will be the key to the final promotion push.

Mackail-Smith, one of those 'young players' rewarded with a more lucrative and extended contract last Friday, fluffed his only opening in the first half, while Mclean failed narrowly to score his 30th goal of the season and thus emulate Peter Price, the last Posh player to surpass that landmark in 1972.

Substitute Charlie Lee's late header that Hoult grasped on the line was their best effort. Joe Lewis's most anxious moment in the Posh goal was a close-range volley from veteran Michael Johnson that left him fearful for his manhood and then counting his good fortune and mercifully intact undercarriage.

Though a historic 'local' rivalry seldom surfaced before Peterborough's second largest League Two crowd of the season of 7,173, the future remains promising for the home team. County, however, slipped closer to the brink of Conference football despite a fine performance that was underpinned by the veterans, Johnson and Hoult.

Their manager Ian McParland has called for his players to be 'warriors', a fitting analogy on the fringes of the Fenlands where that feisty pre-suffragette Boadicea, the warrior queen, careered like a woman chariot driver around the marsh lands of nearby Sawtry and East Anglia.

She had her good days, of course, the best being a resounding home win against the Italians at Colchester, but the Romans, as ever in a tight formation, slaughtered her warriors in the return match somewhere near Nuneaton. Needless to say, it all ended in tears – and Boadicea's suicide by poison.

Superstitious County fans might take note…

Peterborough United (4-4-2): Lewis; Gnakpa, Morgan, Westwood, Day; Low (C Lee 61), Hyde, Keates, Boyd (Rendell 79); Mackail-Smith (Hatch 71), Mclean
Subs: Blackett, McKeown (g).
Booked: none.

Notts County (4-4-2): Hoult; Tann, Edwards, Johnson, Mayo; Butcher, Silk, Smith, Corden (Hunt 90); J Lee, Jarvis (Parkinson 72).

Subs: Canoville, McCann, Weir-Daley.
Booked: Smith.

Referee: R Lewis (Shropshire).

Friday, March 21

MK Dons 1 Peterborough United 1

stadium:mk

Peterborough have the chance to avenge an earlier home defeat by Paul Ince's side and replace them at the top of the table.

AMID an early Easter and Arctic temperatures, normal service remains pleasingly predictable at the summit of League Two.

A club record attendance of 14,521 witnessed a tense but flowing encounter between the leading promotion protagonists in the division at stadium:mk last night. It came as no surprise that the status quo was not disturbed as MK Dons stayed in pole position on goal difference ahead of Peterborough United.

With an appearance at Wembley next Sunday in the Johnstone's Paint Trophy final to anticipate – around 35,000 Milton Kensyans are expected to travel south – the home side seemed likely to add the scalp of their nearest rivals to their successes when Aaron Wilbraham swept the Dons ahead in the 12th minute.

A mistake by Chris Westwood allowed Jemal Johnson progress down the right and his low pass was flicked on by Colin Cameron for Wilbraham to pounce.

The visitors, though, grew in confidence and were worthy of the equaliser that arrived in the 27th minute. Dean Keates floated over a high centre to the far post where Chris Whelpdale dived to good effect and headed firmly into the back of the net.

Above: Chris Whelpdale swoops to conquer, well level, with a splendid diving header from a Dean Keates centre, cancelling out Aaron Wilbraham's earlier effort. The score finished 1-1 and the status quo of Dons top and Posh second remained until the end of the season.

Pics courtesy of the Peterborough Evening Telegraph

Below: Peterborough's prolific forward partnership of Aaron Mclean and Craig Mackail-Smith find Danny Swailes, the MK Dons defender, interrupting their route to goal.

Chances were frequent thereafter with both teams capable of securing a vital win, but none was better than the opening substitute Kevin Gallen screwed wide in time added on at the end. It would have been a cruel blow to the Posh had it squeezed inside the post, however.

MK Dons (4-4-2): Gueret; Diallo (Stirling 82), O'Hanlon, Swailes, Lewington; Dyer, Andrews, Cameron (Livermore 80), Wright (Gallen 63); Wilbraham, Johnson.
Subs: Miles, Abbey (g).
Booked: Andrews.
Goal: Wilbraham (12).

Peterborough United (4-4-2): Lewis; Gnakpa, Morgan, Westwood, Day; Whelpdale, Hyde (Lee 85), Keates, Boyd; Mackail-Smith (Rendell 35), Mclean
Subs: McKeown (g), Blackett, Low.
Booked: Gnakpa, Boyd.
Goal: Whelpdale (27).

Referee: P Walton (Northamptonshire).

POSTSCRIPT: *Peterborough retained second position behind the champions after clinching promotion with two games remaining by beating Hereford 1-0 at Edgar Street.*

Saturday, March 22

Mansfield Town 1 Grimsby Town 2

Field Mill

*Mansfield Town have not won at home since Boxing Day
and the club's internal politics are in no better shape.*

AS the BBC would concur through gritted teeth, Sir Alex
Ferguson is fairly selective about who he talks to these days.

All the more astonishing, then, that the Manchester
United manager should pick up the phone recently and dial
a complete stranger who, on the face of it, was burdened
with a few unwanted problems.

The recipient of the unlikely pro-active Samaritan service
was Stephen Booth, the Mansfield Town chief executive,
who had just announced that the ailing League Two club had
parted company with manager Billy Dearden.

"I was absolutely gratified that Sir Alex had actually given
me a call. He doesn't know me from Adam," said Booth.

Whatever the reason for contact, and there is usually an
ulterior motive in such cases, Ferguson cautioned against
radical change and stressed the virtues of experience when
considering candidates for the vacancy.

In the event, continuity has prevailed with Paul Holland
stepping up from assistant to caretaker-manager, at least until
the end of play today. Sadly, the continuity has extended to
results as Mansfield continue to win away with surprising ease
but are still searching for a first home victory since Boxing Day
after a 2-1 defeat to Grimsby Town at ice station Field Mill.

Booth admits that 'Dutch', the caretaker's inevitable nickname, is the players' choice and performances have improved since he took charge three games ago, although the uncertainty surrounding the club's future lingers on.

A complicated, almost messy affair, Booth is the deal broker who insists the consortium that is buying out owner Keith Haslam is on the brink of finalising finances and that lawyers should conclude business later this week.

News of a Tony Blair apology or permafrost in Hades may break before the deal is rubber-stamped, but while Mansfield folk will not be holding their breath, Booth is adamant that local people, not property developers, will ascend to power.

Somewhere in the boardroom there is a £1 coin, the amount Haslam paid for Mansfield umpteen years ago, that is sufficient to take control of the football club, if not the ground and its surrounding land, which still belongs to Haslam.

To say there is discord among the Mansfield board would be an understatement along the lines that Blair and Gordon Brown were not the best of friends. It is far deeper than that but James Derry, a Newark-based businessman, seems to be growing increasingly impatient with developments, or lack of them.

Derry may well not be the solution at any rate, but what is certain is that Haslam's time is nearly at an end with the Stags. Fans have grown weary of his ownership over the years, but that has evolved into something far nastier, a vitriolic undercurrent that borders on violence, and elements of those feelings, expressed vocally, surfaced once more, even if the target of its abuse was not present, preferring wisely to keep a low profile in trying times.

"Everything is in the hands of the lawyers at the moment," said Booth. "It is a very frustrating period for everyone but I believe that we will have achieved the right thing for Mansfield and the right people for the club, Mansfield-based people, by the time everything is finalised.

"We don't want even to consider the prospect of going down just yet."

Still, the uncertainty of relegation hovers menacingly over Field Mill, a descent to that baffling geometrical abyss – forever lost in a Bermuda Triangle of Blue Square origin wherein clubs are steered completely off course and off the radar until crashing somewhere near the base of the pyramid.

Rent for the stadium will be determined by how far down that structure Mansfield slip and slide and it seems certain that a considerable rebate will be required initially despite a gutsy show of endeavour from the team in yellow.

The talented Peter Till, whose skills should decorate Wembley next Sunday when Grimsby play MK Dons in the Johnstone's Paint Trophy final, squeezed the visitors ahead before a smart turn and finish by Nathan Arnold deservedly levelled. Phil Barnes then denied the same player with a fine save before Danny Boshell twice headed attempts by John Mullins off the line, one against the crossbar, in a frantic period of Mansfield pressure.

Saviour at one end, Boshell then arrowed a smashing shot into the top corner from 20 yards, space created by Till's trickery, to secure the points and nourish Grimsby play-off hopes.

"Going down with the Wrexham" was the less than charitable chant from away fans, a fitting riposte to the Beatles' *Yellow Submarine* tune that had started play. The sinking feeling persists in North Nottinghamshire.

Mansfield Town (4-4-2): White; Mullins, Baptiste, Buxton, Jelleyman; Hamshaw (Louis 83), Dawson, D'Laryea (Horlock 77), W Atkinson (Wainwright 66); Boulding, Arnold.
Subs: Muggleton (g), Briggs.
Booked: Jelleyman.
Goal: Arnold (49).

Grimsby Town (4-3-1-2): Barnes; Clarke, R Atkinson (Bennett 65), Fenton, Newey; Bolland (Jones 65), Boshell, Hegarty; Till; North (Hunt 46), Butler.
Subs: Montgomery (g), Taylor.
Booked: Fenton.
Goals: Till (32), Boshell (74).

Referee: A Hall (West Midlands).

POSTSCRIPT: *It went from bad to worse for the Stags. Off the field, a fantasist by the name of John Batchelor announced he wanted to take over the club and re-name it Harchester United after the fictional dream team on Sky television. Nothing like a bonkers idea linked to celebrity cult to massage an ego, is there? On the field, despite Holland's urgings, performances did not improve and they were denied even the last throw of the dice at Dagenham and Redbridge on the final day of the season, already relegated when Chester drew with Stockport after Mansfield's home defeat to Rotherham United. Thirty years after their predecessors had performed at a hitherto unprecedented Second Division level for the North Nottinghamshire club, Mansfield slipped tamely away and relinquished a precious league status without a whimper.*

Monday March 24

Nottingham Forest 0 Brighton 0

City Ground

*Forest attempt to revive their diminishing hopes
of automatic promotion against an exhausted Brighton
trapped in the grip of fearful fixture congestion.*

AS the county braces itself to mourn the loss of at least one its football clubs to the non-league pyramid, Nottingham Forest should also be preparing for bad news come the end of the season.

A goalless draw with Brighton and Hove Albion at the City Ground yesterday was the latest in a disappointing sequence that has secured just one victory in six games. Any hopes of automatic promotion have virtually evaporated as Carlisle United's impressive form continues unabated, hoisting the Cumbrians 11 points clear of Forest.

The visitors were well worth the point that moved them into sixth position above Tranmere Rovers on goals scored, and with the teams below them striving to improve, even Forest's task of repeating last May's effort of reaching the play-offs may be in jeopardy with trips to Doncaster Rovers and Carlisle to negotiate in the next seven days.

This was Brighton's eighth game in 24 days, their ninth inside a month follows at the weekend against Leeds United, currently relaxing in Spain. "It's crazy that we have to play nearly a quarter of our season in a month," said Brighton manager Dean Wilkins, who was nonetheless pleased with the effort of his young but clearly fatigued squad.

Had Dean Forster not squandered an early sitter Brighton might have prevailed, although Matt Thornhill was similarly profligate with an open goal midway through the second half.

Paul Smith's only other scare in the Forest goal was when he tipped Tommy Elphick's close range header onto the crossbar, but Michel Kuipers also thwarted Kris Commons early on and when the Dutch goalkeeper was beaten, by Brett Ormerod and Lewis McGugan, the post intervened to deny Forest a crucial advantage.

Nottingham Forest (4-4-2): Smith;
Chambers (McCleary 74), Morgan, Wilson, Bennett;
Thornhill (McGugan 74), Clingan, Cohen (Agogo 84),
Commons; Ormerod, Tyson.
Subs: Sinclair, Byrne.
Booked: Cohen.

Brighton and Hove Albion (4-4-2): Kuipers; Hart,
Elphick, Lynch, Mayo; Thomson (Loft 69), Racon,
Cox (Butters 90), Martot; Forster (Robinson 74), Murray.
Subs: Gatting, McFaul.
Booked: Hart, Thomson.

Referee: N Miller (Durham).

POSTSCRIPT: *Brighton's travails saw the south coast club eventually run out of steam and, curiously, their chairman run out of patience with manager Dean Wilkins, who was replaced by old boy Micky Adams. Forest, with six wins in their final seven games, surged into the second automatic promotion place in a dramatic denouement on the season's final day. They held out to beat Yeovil, their nemesis in the play-off semi finals the previous season, while Doncaster's defeat at Cheltenham saw Forest sneak into the runners-up position.*

Sunday, March 30

MK Dons 2 Grimsby Town 0

Wembley Stadium

The Johnstone's Paint Trophy celebrates the 25th anniversary of what was the Football League Trophy by throwing together the old and the new for its first final at the revamped Wembley.

WHEN asked recently if the club had any players of advancing years to form a side to play in charity matches, an MK Dons official answered positively. "We have a few, but they're all in the first team," he said, responding to the 60-something Peterborough United old boy who was keen to start a series of matches with their League Two promotion rivals on the veterans' circuit.

Re-invented scarcely five years ago, the club is a mere novice in the relatively ancient environs of the Football League. Even in doggie years, they remain pups among some faithful old retrievers, so it's unlikely that many of their playing staff will be relying on their pensions, which can be drawn at 35 years of age, just yet.

Such is the assured vibrancy of youth, an elixir that MK Dons possess in abundance and one that was enough to secure this embryonic club its first glimmer of silverware by beating Grimsby Town 2-0 in the Johnstone's Paint Trophy final yesterday.

The return to Wembley II, after a sabbatical in Cardiff, failed to inspire a classic encounter, certainly nothing to compare with the Doncaster-Bristol Rovers epic of last year, a relentlessly pulsating affair that provided a riveting farewell to the Millennium Stadium for domestic showcase finals.

Still, a crowd of 56,615 represents the second best at a football match in the UK this weekend, higher than the Auld Firm duel in Glasgow, and further vindication of this competition which is avoided by players and fans like a recurring social disease in its early stages but is embraced like a bonnie baby's head during Election week as the final looms into sight.

Over half that attendance made the short journey from Milton Keynes, a voyage of adventure and discovery for the new town. "Here luv, don't shout, we don't get out too much," was how one of its female residents explained it when asked to move along by police at Wembley Park railway station.

There is also justification for Pete Winkelman, the expansive Dons chairman who uprooted Wimbledon, the club's previous incarnation, to Milton Keynes five years ago then changed its name a year later, inciting criticism for daring to use that dirty 'F' word known as franchise.

"It doesn't get much better than this," said Winkelman, who may find a few dissenters in the Wimbledon camp of 1988 that claimed the FA Cup from Liverpool.

It was scarcely a surprise that the Dons should adapt more adroitly to unfamiliar environs after moving stadia three times in the last five years. Set against that, Grimsby were formed in 1878, the same year that Cleopatra's Needle ended its torturous journey from Alexandria to the Thames Embankment. It was also the year that a few gallant Welshmen saw off Zulus revolting at Rorke's Drift, with the sun still shining brightly on the Empire.

That star was setting by the time Grimsby moved to Blundell Park, in 1899, where they have been rooted ever since. The trawler industry has come and gone, as did Jeff Whitefoot, a former Busby Babe who once said he must have been under 'hypnosis' when he decided to move from Old Trafford to Cleethorpes in 1957.

Among its most notable sporting sons have been Duncan McKenzie, the Mini-hopping, golf ball hurling and all-round wizard of the wing extraordinaire whose talents lit up Nottingham Forest, Mansfield Town, Leeds United and Everton but never Sir Alf Ramsey's England, curiously enough.

Those who felt it should have been a day for the purists and football traditionalists rather than upstart young critters with masters from the world of rock and popular music most probably endured that sinking feeling from the game's opening gambits.

When Danny North scuffed an early chance, then Danny Boshell's limp penalty was saved by Willy Gueret after the Dons goalkeeper had felled Paul Bolland in the 18th minute, it seemed increasingly inevitable that the new money would prevail over the ancient, in comparison, Mariners. So it proved.

A frantic goalmouth scramble shortly after half-time saw Colin Cameron's shot ricochet off the post where Sean O'Hanlon's follow-up was denied supremely by Phil Barnes' reactions before Nick Hegarty pushed Danny Swailes in the back. Captain Keith Andrews did not shirk his responsibility, converting the spot kick with aplomb before O'Hanlon's header, deflected onwards by Rob Atkinson, from Cameron's 81st minute corner, settled the 25th anniversary final.

For the winners' high-profile fledgling manager Paul Ince, this is a gratifying step in the right direction, if only a small one. He has already stated that he has turned down offers to join Championship clubs, thus confirming his intent to manage at the same level with his current employers.

With promotion virtually certain, though, the thoughts of Brian Clough may offer more encouragement. The great manager, who won two European Cups and a First Division title with Nottingham Forest, recalled that his most significant City Ground trophy was the first he won with them.

It was the Anglo-Scottish Cup – another 'Mickey Mouse' trophy but one cherished by Clough – a now defunct competition that expired unloved and unlamented... south of the border at any rate.

Should MK Dons have ideas above their station, inspiration is at hand from those achievements of Clough and indeed Wimbledon.

A few years on the clock and the Premier League may yet be in reach – as well as raising a decent veterans' team before the remainder are all dead and buried.

Grimsby Town (3-5-2): Barnes; Atkinson, Fenton, Newey; Clarke, Bolland, Hunt (Toner 79), Boshell, Hegarty; North (Bore 46) Till (Jones 61).
Subs: Bennett, Montgomery (g).
Booked: Boshell.

MK Dons (4-5-1): Gueret; Stirling, O'Hanlon, Swailes, Lewington; Dyer, Navarro, Andrews, Cameron (Baldock 90), Johnson (Wright 77); Gallen (Wilbraham 77).
Subs: Edds, Abbey (g).
Booked: Navarro.
Goals: Andrews (74 pen), O'Hanlon (81).

Referee: P Joslin (Nottinghamshire).

Saturday, April 5

Swansea City 1 Bournemouth 2

Liberty Stadium

*Swansea need a win and a defeat for
Doncaster Rovers to secure promotion.*

AS Gordon Brown knows full well, it is not just the gatecrashers who can spoil a party. Bad enough that some of your own uninvited guests are conspiring against the cause and seeking a premature end to the fun and games, but when one of the opposition, who might otherwise be expected to display a certain allegiance, suddenly floors you with a surprise show of hands, it is time to unplug the Speaker and clear the House to avoid further damage.

In the case of Joe Partington, it was a show of heads – his own actually – in the 90th minute that knocked the stuffing out of Swansea City and emptied the Liberty Stadium in rapid fashion on Saturday.

Since Partington represents Wales at Under-19 level, a sense of Fifth Columnist betrayal may well have gnawed away at entrenched partisans in the ground.

His first senior goal ruined the League One leaders' promotion celebrations as Bournemouth secured a vital 2-1 victory, their fourth in five games, to sustain their own unlikely version of the great escape.

With Doncaster Rovers hauling themselves level late on at Huddersfield, it transpired that Swansea could not have claimed a Championship berth anyway and Jo Kuffour's winner from a counter attack two minutes into injury time merely compounded the Gower gloom.

'Surreal' was how Bournemouth manager Kevin Bond described the finale. Departing Swansea fans espoused alternatives.

A belated 18th birthday bash with his family awaited Partington at the weekend, attended by his Welsh mother Tina, the biological reason that her teenage son, born in Portsmouth, is captain of the Wales Under-19 side.

His equaliser from a Warren Cummings corner arrived less than two minutes after being sent on as a substitute with instructions from the bench to 'make yourself a nuisance at set-pieces'!

Clearly an attentive lad who obeys orders, young Partington.

In fact, this was only his second goal this season, the other, also a header, scored for the Welsh in Hungary.

"Someone headed me from behind and when I came round, they told me I had scored," recalled Partington. "So I'm glad I've got one I can remember!" The Welsh contingent at the Liberty will not forget it in a hurry.

In the dressing room corridors, a partisan voice of Rhondda origin told the young centre half that 'you'll never play for Wales again, lad', a laughing rebuke from Alan Curtis, highly-respected coach and something of a mentor to Partington and his other charges in the Wales FA youth teams.

A former Wales international, Curtis enjoys legendary status with Swansea, evoking their First Division exploits of the 1980s which ushered in a season of unprecedented success, a sixth-place finish and a place in Europe guaranteed with resorting to hammering Bangor in the Welsh Cup final.

Ironically, those heady days savoured by Curtis and his colleagues were merely prelude to a dramatic fall from grace.

That descent saw them tumble from top to bottom in four seasons, but reparation of sorts is almost a formality when, rather than if, the current squad – by general consensus the best in this section by a country mile – restore Championship status for the first time in 24 years.

It seemed inevitable when Andy Robinson's header from Thomas Butler's corner steered Swansea in front, even if Bournemouth's defending constituted gross dereliction of duty as the ball rolled over the line inside a far post unguarded by a covering defender.

News that Doncaster were trailing filtered around terraces rejoicing in harmony about the present state of affairs and a future in elevated company. They even brought out the Brandy, on-loan Manchester United forward Febian, to add to the intoxicating atmosphere. Alas, no cigar. And the champagne? Like the *Titanic* which sailed on its tragic maiden voyage from Southampton 96 years ago this month, that must remain on ice.

There were moments when destiny seemed in Swansea's favour, however, driven on as they were by Leon Britton, industrious and inventive in equal measure in a midfield where Darren Anderton's consummate ability eclipsed his bursting lungs during his first match in five months.

However, David Forde was to be their nemesis in the Bournemouth goal, particularly in the 67th minute when in quick succession he denied Robinson, Brandy and Butler, which on reflection could shape up to be a respectable name for a City law firm one day.

Earlier profligacy was beginning to erode confidence at the back but, with only minutes remaining, Kuffour's right-foot effort from 20 yards rebounded up and away off the crossbar and seemingly with it, Bournemouth's chances of rescuing a point.

A game of snakes and ladders, ups and downs, ended with both sides
still anchored in League One. Darryl Duffy and Jason Pearce
grapple with the basics of ball control.

Pic courtesy of Huw Evans agency

Perhaps the team coach that transported them from the
south coast should have revealed a clue as to the visitors'
salvation, a bus run by a company known as Bluebird travel,
not the most popular feathered friend in these parts when in
the plural. Of course the Bluebirds, Cardiff City's nickname,
also reached their first FA Cup final since 1927 yesterday by
beating Barnsley, so a good weekend for anything sporting
blue and drawn to air travel to pack away the wings or duck
when flying low over the Liberty.

Should they prevail in what must be the divisional title
decider, at second-placed Carlisle United tomorrow night,
Swansea manager Roberto Martinez's mission will just about
be accomplished. In some style, too, it has to be said.

Somewhere sitting in the ground was the millionth spectator who had passed through the turnstiles since the stadium opened in 2005, but it is only in the last 12 months that the imagination has been fired by Martinez's calculated cavalier tactics, wonderfully embodied by the rampaging Spaniard and phonetically-friendly Angel Rangel, a right back who does not seek permission from the bench when crossing the halfway line to join in attack.

For Bournemouth, the battle against relegation and financial implosion goes on. The campaign to avoid both remains bleak.

It has been a long road for Bond this season, including a nasty scare at Holker Street in the first round of the FA Cup when elimination might have cost him his job. At Barrow, where a 1-1 draw and then narrow replay victory elicited boardroom loyalty, his father John turned up to lend moral support, a charismatic figure in his pomp fondly recalled in the match-day programme during his managerial attempts to reverse the ebbing tide at Swansea as they wallowed at the foot of Third Division in the ominous year of 1984 (if only then Mankind had known that Big Brother would eventually rule the world through a small cathode tube and a watertight patent, maybe it could have been averted).

Though the task would have defeated King Canute, his exertions clearly were appreciated by the author of the piece, Peter Jones, brother of comedian Rob Brydon.

In an era when football managers and chairman seemed to merge into a hybrid of Arthur Daley and Lew Grade, Bond's cigar chomping entrance from his flash 'Jag' impressed locals and players alike, both of whom relied on more conservative modes of transport and Woodbines rather than expensive Havanas.

Unable to speak Rafael Benitez-Spanish or Arsene Wenger-English fluently, and without the luxury of rotation and foreign players, Bond at least kept the wolves at bay for a season at Swansea before his departure shortly before Christmas a year after his appointment. Jones remembers as a young lad being so 'choked' by his dismissal that he could not finish his chip butty in Ray's Chip Shop in Neath – 'and they were damn good butties' lamented Jones with double sorrow.

Strangely, there is a familiar comparison to Bond Snr in his son's plight, a club in financial crisis and trying to avoid a disastrous drop to the league basement being the most transparent similarity. Bournemouth, however, are even deeper in the maelstrom. A ten-point deduction for entering administration has all but relegated the club, while the players accepting a 50 per-cent reduction in salary has dented confidence. Not morale, though – on the pitch, as recent results have confirmed, and certainly not on the terraces.

With their team in arrears and Doncaster trailing, the 226 travelling band in the West Stand, many of whom had travelled from the south coast in the wee small hours and back with the sun rising once again to witness the FA Cup draw at Barrow, struck up a chorus.

Que sera, sera, whatever will be, will be; we're going to Shrewsbury, que sera, sera.

Not quite as stirring as *Men of Harlech*.

Yet such stoic resignation surely deserves greater reward – and bigger and more appreciative audiences.

Swansea City: (4-4-2): De Vries; Rangel, Tate, Lawrence, Austin; Butler (Tudur-Jones 77), Britton, Pratley, Robinson; Scotland (Bauza 86), Duffy (Brandy 59)
Subs: Way, Williams.
Booked: Auston, De Vries, Tate.
Goal: Robinson 50.

Bournemouth: (4-5-1): Forde; Bradbury, Gowling, Pearce, Cummings; Kuffour, Cooper, Anderton (Partington 88), Tessem (Pitman 59), Gradel; Vokes (Garry 90).
Subs: Pryce (g), McQuoid.
Booked: Pearce.
Goals: Partington (90), Kuffour (90).

Referee: M Haywood (West Yorkshire).

Saturday, April 12

Gillingham 1 Swansea City 2

Priestfield Stadium

Victory for the visitors can clinch promotion while
plunging Gillingham deeper into the mire.

EVEN the most recalcitrant of managers steeped in a prejudice inspired by the colour of their own team's shirt would agree on one thing. The table never lies. Ask Basil Fawlty or his alter ego, Arsene Wenger.

Confirmation of that old adage that brings harmony to the managerial inner sanctum was provided by Swansea City's joyful promotion at Priestfield on Saturday.

Another universal truth, at least acknowledged in League One, surely will also be confirmed when the Welsh club claim the divisional title before the end of the season, thus vindicating the general belief that Roberto Martinez's side have been the best by far at this level for some months now.

It was on a dank Tuesday night at their Liberty Stadium last November that Swansea established pole position on goal difference from Leyton Orient with a solitary goal victory over Hartlepool United.

Despite the close attentions of several pretenders to that throne, including Nottingham Forest, Carlisle United and Doncaster Rovers, Swansea continued to consolidate then distance themselves from the chasing pack, the zenith during a period of splendid football being a rapturously received rout of Leeds United two days before the turn of the year. That with Swansea reduced to ten men before half-time.

That win over Hartlepool was secured by full-back Angel Rangel's late effort, and in a pleasing symmetry, his compatriot Guillem Bauza, the first of three Spaniards acquired by Martinez last summer, scored both goals as Swansea recovered to beat Gillingham 2-1 and serve notice to the Championship of their presence when play commences next August.

Dennis Oli's opener deservedly had the relegation strugglers in front as the home team applied a pressure that should have at least doubled that advantage, but for the errant finishing of Simeon Jackson and Oli himself.

Last week it was a belated double whammy delivered by Bournemouth that deflated Swansea ambitions, two goals in as many minutes in stoppage time bringing defeat and shameful red faces all around in south Wales.

Football's nature, though, has a curious way of maintaining a delicate balance and Bauza, or Bussy as Swansea staff call him, steered a way through the home defence with a couple of swift goals, the second a sweet half volley, in two frantic minutes shortly before the interval.

Initially Gillingham contested them both, one for a perceived foul on their goalkeeper and the second for hand ball by the scorer, but on reflection their manager Mark Stimson agreed that both were legitimate finishes.

Leaving Martinez to enjoy the moment, a job well done and lavish praise on his squad. "Normally you get your rewards over a season and we have maintained the level of performance and standards we set out to keep in July," said Martinez. "That has been the key to our success.

"If you look at the fans' faces at the end there, they deserve this and so do the players. We have waited 24 years for this and they [the fans and players] should be proud of themselves."

Certainly 'style' has been a word synonymous with Swansea's resurgence, largely thanks to Martinez, who joined the club as a player on a short-term contract in January 2003 as it was in danger of tumbling out of the league.

Desperate times for Swansea, as recalled by Colin Addison, their manager in 2002, who watched the decline with impotent disbelief after a Londoner named Tony Petty had bought the club for £1 – with ruinous consequences.

"I called him Potty," recalled Addison, a radio pundit nowadays, but formerly a fleet-footed inside forward with Nottingham Forest during the 1960s and, more famously, the man who guided Hereford United to their finest two hours when beating Newcastle United, after extra time, in the FA Cup third round replay in 1972.

"On his first morning in charge, he called me into his office and told me to find the six best paid players, tell them they are sacked and rip up their contracts. Before training. Lunacy."

If Martinez played a significant role in survival that season he was eclipsed, as were all others in a Swansea shirt, by local boy James Thomas, whose hat trick during a 4-2 victory over Hull City at the old Vetch Field preserved league membership on the final day of the season.

Five years with Martinez at the head of affairs, 86 points represents a new club record, surpassing the John Hollins promotion tally that took the Swans up as champions from Division Three in 2000.

With Ospreys triumphant at Twickenham at the weekend and Cardiff striving to win at Wembley next month in the FA Cup final, no surprise that a small corner of Kent should be conquered by the Welsh at the full time whistle.

Swansea manager Roberto Martinez was able to celebrate promotion at Priestfield. "The players should be proud of themselves," the Spaniard said. Certainly he could be proud of his own unerring devotion to playing the game in a manner which entertained, enthralled and engaged audiences. It also won the odd match or two along the way.

Pics courtesy of Huw Evans agency

Confronted by just a few policemen re-enforced by yapping dogs rather than 5,000 Zulus armed with spears and rifles, *Men of Harlech* was replaced by *Land of My Fathers*, belted out by a 1,500-strong choir and beamed back, as was the match, to a similarly appreciative audience sat in luxury corporate seats at the Liberty.

Not since 1984 have Swansea performed in the second tier when John Bond kept them afloat for one season before being sacked at Christmas, his departure as inevitable as the team's eventual demotion that summer, followed with indecent haste by a further relegation to the bottom level the following year.

A cigar-smoking, champagne-fuelled figure of fond recollection, Bond seems almost a Neanderthal in the game today, particularly when Martinez takes centre stage.

Modish and self-effacing, and appearing trim enough to stroll 90 minutes at this level even today, he hugged every one of his players at the end of the match and waited patiently as the fans paid homage behind the goal they had been attacking in the second half.

The usual celebrations, some topless dancing and Klinsmann-esque theatricals in the penalty area ensued, but amidst the high jinks, the little Spaniard calmly busied himself responding to media demands for television, radio and newspaper interviews out on the pitch.

There have been shades of Scunthorpe's hugely successful and equally runaway promotion that captured the imagination last season. Different strokes, of course, as a formidable team spirit rather than flowing movement prevailed. That and the daunting prospect of turning out at Glanford Park did for most opponents with anything less than a strong stomach for a fight and solid constitution.

As Scunthorpe romped to the title last year, they sang about their physio, Nigel Adkin, being better than Mourinho. Swansea fans have revived the tune but chant only the manager's name in harmonious homage. No comparison necessary.

As Scunthorpe all but bade farewell to the Championship at the weekend, further comparisons with the wilting Iron may also be unfounded.

At least that's the hope in Swansea.

Gillingham (3-5-2): Stillie; Richards, Cullip, King; Southall (Pugh 85), Crofts, Maher, Miller (Griffiths 66), Fuller; Oli (Simmonds 75), Jackson.
Subs: Kiely (g), Clohessy.
Booked: Maher, Miller.
Goal: Oli (22).

Swansea City: (4-4-2): De Vries; Tate, Williams, Lawrence, Painter; Anderson, Pratley, Britton, Robinson (Butler 73); Bauza (Tudur-Jones 90), Scotland (Brandy 77).
Subs: Austin, Way, Williams.
Booked: Pratley, Bauza, Painter, Britton.
Goals: Bauza (44, 45).

Referee: C Penton (Sussex).

POSTSCRIPT: *Swansea suffered another home defeat, to Yeovil, the following week, but with Carlisle also losing, to Southend United, the Welshmen were able to claim the title. Well almost. Leeds United's case to have their 15 points reinstated was still in abeyance and the League refused to allow Swansea to be presented with the trophy until it was resolved. On May 1, an independent panel upheld the League's disciplinary action. Leeds were denied restoration of even a single point and Swansea's championship season was official - at last.*

Tuesday, April 15

MK Dons 0 Hereford United 0

stadium:mk

*MK Dons require a win to confirm promotion,
although a draw would virtually guarantee it anyway.*

PAUL INCE'S managerial CV, small but perfectly formed like the player he was, welcomed another impressive entry as MK Dons claimed the draw with Hereford United that effectively secured promotion.

Fourth-placed Stockport County, whom they play on Saturday, can equal their points tally, but given the disparity in goal difference, the Dons can prepare for next season in League One. Even so, celebrations were distinctly muted at stadium:mk last night.

Never mind that the transport of delight which has ferried them to the top of the table and Wembley appears to be running out of petrol, Ince – who rescued Macclesfield from the relegation abyss last season – should be adding the divisional title to the Johnstone's Paint Trophy that was lifted last month to his achievements in charge of a club that was only created five years ago.

Hereford also consolidated their own automatic promotion aspirations. Their roots are rather more historic than the Dons but in this their second season back in the League, their elevation would be equally welcome.

Devoid of passion and pace, the game meandered curiously as Lloyd Dyer and Jemal Johnson posed the scant menace in a soulless first half, a couple of attempts that Wayne Brown dealt with comfortably enough.

Hereford were no better. Their forays over the halfway line scarcely offered anything but a token offensive and only the combination of Gary Hooper and Clint Easton, just a whisker away from a famous Hollywood pairing, seemed able to unsettle the Dons back four. It was Hooper's 25th minute header, deflected wide of the post, that was as close as the visitors came to an opener.

A speculative effort from Jude Stirling caught the mood of things. The big full-back released a powerful left-foot shot that fleetingly stirred the home crowd before it fell to earth close to the corner flag – for a Hereford throw.

An injection of urgency into the league leaders' tactics increased a hitherto languid tempo and it nearly reaped its reward when Alan Navarro's 20-yard shot squirted across the damp surface where Brown pushed it wide for a corner.

Just after the hour, though, the Dons should have been ahead. A flowing movement typical of their style presented Dyer with a simple task from ten-yards out that he plonked limply over the crossbar.

With pressure mounting, Mark Wright was denied by Toumani Diagouraga on the line, but despite a flourish at the end, Hereford held firm for a valuable point.

MK Dons (4-4-2): Gueret; Stirling, O'Hanlon, Swailes, Lewington; Dyer, Navarro, Andrews, J Johnson (Wright 59); Wilbraham, Miles (Gallen 87). **Subs:** Regan, Abbey (g), Hadfield.

Hereford United (4-4-2): Brown; McClenahan, Broadhurst, Beckwith, Rose; S Johnson, Diagouraga, Smith, Easton; Hooper (Robinson 59), Guinan (Taylor 79).

Subs: Esson (g), Gwynne, Collins.
Booked: Hooper.

Referee: S Tanner (Somerset).

POSTSCRIPT: *MK Dons duly confirmed their promotion with a stirring 3-2 win at play-off contenders Stockport County, twice retrieving a goal deficit to sneak victory. The following weekend, an 18th away win of the season, equalling a league record, a 2-1 victory over Bradford City, secured the title. Paul Ince, after declining offers of Championship management earlier in the season finally found Premier League Blackburn Rovers too big a temptation and was appointed as Mark Hughes' replacement in June... Hereford's 3-0 win at Brentford on the penultimate weekend of the season brought a second promotion in two seasons after previously being absent in the Conference for nine years.*

Saturday, April 19

Wrexham 1 Notts County 0

Racecourse Ground

Defeat for Wrexham by one of their relegation rivals would send them down to the Blue Square Premier.

THEY came not to praise Wrexham, but to bury them. Vulnerable at the back, a single, swift and penetrating attack would have floored the Welsh club and ended a love affair with the Football League that began in 1921.

The mourners, though, even those who trudged to the Racecourse Ground fearing the worst for their own side, should have known better of a team that has raised relegation-dodging to an art form.

Riding their luck on a pitch blighted with more bumps than Hugh Hefner's swimming pool, Wrexham eked out a 1-0 victory over a hapless and equally-troubled Notts County to delay their exile from League Two for at least another week.

Et tu, Wrexham? Not just yet.

A fatal blow, however, could be inflicted at Edgar Street tomorrow night by a Hereford United determined to secure an automatic promotion. With Dagenham and Redbridge playing Mansfield Town on the last day of the season, a defeat over the Welsh border would confirm Wrexham's relegation and vanquish any hope springing eternal in North Wales that a second great escape to eclipse last year's final day triumph over Boston United can be achieved.

It is a remote prospect. Even their manager Brian Little had been talking in concerned tones and preparing players and fans alike for the Blue Square experience, although if their remaining opponents turn up armed with plastic knives and a predatory instinct as blunted as County's, the mission might yet be accomplished.

Danny Crow was most profligate for the visitors during a dreadful contest that cruelly illustrated Wrexham's status at the bottom of the table and County's three places above but still uncertain as to their own fate.

"We have become acclimatised to going down but it won't be the end of the world if we do," assured Geraint Parry, Wrexham's football secretary, who admits that he still might shed a tear should his worst fears be realised.

For Parry, though, it is a labour of love. Thirty years ago, he left school and hopped on a train from Birkenhead to see a Wrexham team inspired by Mickey Thomas and managed by John Neal play in the old Third Division. He was smitten.

"When I left school, I started to write for the programme. Then I joined the Merchant Navy and used to tune in to the World Service to hear how they had got on."

He started compiling the club's website when he returned home, but as backroom staff disappeared at an alarming rate, his role transformed during the Denis Smith era when administration became a financial expediency and extinction seemed an almost unavoidable consequence.

Between writing pen pictures for internet surfers, Parry learned the art of talking to an insolvency expert about the logistics of the first team staying in a hotel overnight before an FA Cup first round tie with Hayes. That was in November 2004, as the club lurched from catastrophe to crisis with a seamless dexterity.

The cast may have changed around Parry but the underlying theme of farce and dramatic content of dark realism endures at the Racecourse.

"I remember seeing fans of Halifax when they dropped out of the league and saw them crying and wondered if I would do the same. We'll see."

Should they tumble, where once there were six Welsh clubs in the Football League, only Swansea and Cardiff will remain, ironically both flourishing in League One and the FA Cup respectively. Wrexham would join compatriots Aberdare Athletic, Merthyr Town and Newport County in adding an unwanted legacy to their club records.

History certainly coursed through this game between the oldest league club in Wales and the oldest league club in the world, staged on the oldest international ground, over 130 years, still in existence on the planet.

Bags of nostalgia from Tommy Lawton to Mickey Thomas but scarcely a trace of the beautiful game. Local lad Neil Roberts won it with a far post finish from a Wes Baynes free kick in the 77th minute, while Gavin Ward denied Jason Lee a leveller shortly after with a fine athletic save from his header.

In short, that was about it. County manager Ian McParland bemoaned a lack of professionalism in certain areas of his team, but the truth is he has inherited a weak squad and an even weaker regime, the Supporters' Trust, that purports to run affairs at Meadow Lane.

It is unthinkable that such a grand old club should be reduced to such an ignominious state, the second occasion in their seasons that their relegation travails are extending until a nerve-shredding denouement at the season's climax.

Wrexham, though, are on familiar territory here.

The first drugs tests to be performed at the Racecourse this season delayed one or two players on their journey home.

For Parry, it was a reminder of how the ground is cherished by the Welsh international side, whose Under-21 team are frequent visitors for representative games.

"It [the drugs testing area] will be up to Uefa standard shortly and we have a fantastic Centre of Excellence and facilities to match," Parry said, before slipping into a premature obituary for his beloved club.

"I just hope the Football League will look at us as being good members and be proud of us. If we do drop down, there will be no big heads or egos. We are getting crowds of around 6,000 for some home games and have a great catchment area. People come from all over Wales to see us and I hope they will continue to do the same, whether we are playing Shrewsbury or Chester in the league or Histon or Kettering in the Conference.

"Carlisle and Lincoln and now Hereford have shown that you can come back and we have to be positive. Mind you, the League's AGM for chairman is normally held in Portugal before the start of a new season. I think the Conference hold theirs in Blackpool, so there might be a few shocks for the board in that respect."

Wrexham (4-4-2): Ward; Pejic, S Evans,
Mike Williams, Taylor; Baynes, Mackin (D Williams 71),
Fleming (Murtagh 71), Done (G Evans 90);
Roberts, Marc Williams.
Subs: Proctor, Jones.
Booked: Baynes, Pejic.
Goal: Roberts (77).

Notts County (4-4-2): Hoult; Canoville, Edwards,
Johnson (Mayo 46), Hunt; Jarvis (Corden 86), Mackenzie,
Butcher, Weston; Crow (Dudfield 52), Lee
Subs: Tann, Weir-Daley.
Booked: Canoville.

Referee: A Bates (Staffordshire).

POSTSCRIPT: *Geraint Parry's expansive eulogy on remaining positive in the Blue Square Premier was as apposite as it was prophetic. A midweek 3-0 defeat at Hereford relegated Wrexham, whereupon Brian Little immediately vowed to restore their status.*

Bad news in North Wales for Wrexham - meanwhile in the south better tidings as Swansea are confirmed champions despite a home defeat to Yeovil, their second in succession following the defeat by Bournemouth. A week later, Paul Anderson celebrates his goal as Swansea end their home fixtures with an emphatic 4-1 win over Leyton Orient on April 26.

Pics courtesy of Huw Evans agency

Saturday, April 26

Bournemouth 1 Crewe Alexandra 0

Dean Court

*Bournemouth must win to avoid relegation, while at
Chelsea, Manchester United lose the game and Rio
Ferdinand loses the plot by 'accidentally' kicking
a female steward in the tunnel.*

JEFF MOSTYN faces something of a quandary this weekend,
exposed to the sort awkward predicament any loving parent
dreads.

"It is the most amazing dilemma," the Bournemouth
chairman said with an air of resignation after his team's most
amazing form had secured a 1-0 victory against Crewe
Alexandra.

The fanfare to celebrate the League One side's final home
game had scarcely subsided, Dean Court's second largest
crowd of the season trooping away bathed in glorious
sunshine and brimming with unbridled optimism.

The win over one of their relegation rivals was their
seventh in eight games that has transformed a club whose
destiny pointed towards the League basement after suffering
a ten-point penalty imposed for entering administration in
February.

Since an away defeat to Gillingham in March, however,
six successive wins have carried Bournemouth to the brink of
perhaps football's greatest escape – and Mostyn to the brink
of family crisis.

While Bournemouth oppose Carlisle United on Saturday at 3pm for a game that could prove their salvation, another match of the day kicks off in Basingstoke an hour earlier. Janine Mostyn's wedding.

"The vicar has already told me he will perform the service on the pitch at Carlisle," Mostyn laughed. "I'll be listening to the vows, but more importantly listening in to the transistor radio for the score.

"I can imagine *Here Comes the Bride* being played as she comes down the aisle and I'm shouting out something about the team news from the radio."

While Mostyn's family devotion is certain to prevail, there is further irony. By Saturday he may well be the proud father walking his daughter down the aisle but he may not be the proud chairman of Bournemouth.

Two consortia, one which includes Mostyn, have a noon deadline today to present bids to the administrator for consideration.

"I have been here 18 months, since I met the previous owner Abdul Jaffer for lunch in Manchester with Kevin Bond (the manager and friend of Mostyn's).

"I have known Kevin for nearly 30 years and I suppose I ended up a bit like Victor Kayam, I liked the business so much I decided to buy it. But it's been the most expensive meal I have ever had in my life!

"I didn't realise just how bad the finances were and I think there were a lot of hidden things behind what was termed disclosure. By the time things unravelled, I was far too ensconced to get out of it, frankly.

"Yes, it has been a nightmare at times and an absolute mess and probably I have regretted getting involved on most occasions, but these sort of days make it worthwhile.

"Administrators are a law unto themselves but I hope to be part of this club and take it forward."

Before and after: Above, Sam Vokes runs to the crowd
in the corner behind the goal where he has just put his side
ahead against Crewe Alexandra...

Pic courtesy of Michael Cunningham

...And below, somewhere beneath that lot is Vokes
whose finish claimed a precious victory and prolonged
the dream of an astonishing escape act.

Mostyn can claim with some justification to be a chairman who has made a difference during his tenure. Even fans have shown their warm appreciation with standing ovations during this latest saga, particularly before one game recently when Mostyn thought it would be his last in charge until, rather predictably in these cases, an offer to take over fell short of funds and failed at the 11th hour.

No wonder he has likened events to a soap opera, although the team's unswerving ability to collect victories and reverse previous form has taken on the air of the surreal lately.

Where the next twist in the script lies largely depends on others now. The result at Brunton Park next Saturday is paramount, as are the ones at Cheltenham, Crewe and Gillingham's away to Leeds, a convoluted finale galvanised by Bournemouth's extraordinary recovery.

The renaissance has evoked memories of a famous, at least this side of the New Forest, scramble to safety under Mel Machin's management, when two wins in the last two games preserved their status in League One in 1995. Victory away at Brentford and a final day 3-0 home win over Shrewsbury before a heaving Dean Court did the trick.

Six years later, Sean O'Driscoll's side sailed to nine wins in the last 12 games of the season that hoisted Bournemouth to within touching distance of an unlikely play-off place in the same division.

In fact, they were just a few short moments from success before a Reading equaliser two minutes from time forced a 3-3 draw and dashed hopes of further progress.

If that sequence was galvanised by a young on-loan forward by the name of Jermain Defoe, pivotal to this current revival has been Sam Vokes, a name bandied about generously by Premier League scouts. Even those at Portsmouth, whose manager Harry Redknapp was a spectator, fondly recalled as he is for his popular and highly successful stewardship of the club in the 1980s.

The 18-year-old embodies many of the traditional centre forward's virtues, robust, brave, marginally nimble on his feet and brave when the boots are flying, although only the most important of assets, a predatory instinct, was required to finish the job and Crewe.

A dreadful defensive header by Danny O'Donnell put his colleagues on the back foot and Vokes in an opposing mode, allowing him to score the only goal of the game, his 12th of the season, a left foot finish that was a fitting punishment, in the 55th minute.

Nervous tension ensued as Nicky Maynard's effort was disallowed, a slightly suspect decision, and David Forde's acrobatics denied distance shots from George Abbey and Dean Morgan.

Referee Keith Hill's whistle for a free-kick in stoppage time signalled a pitch invasion by the cretin factor hugging the touchline, enraging some Crewe players who thought the ending premature. It was a point they continued to dispute with the Hertfordshire official in the tunnel as participants dashed to avoid the gathering hordes. Rather more vigorously than might have been expected, according to eye-witnesses, as Hill was restrained forcibly by some of the visitors.

"Pinned against the wall" was the unofficial version from anonymous kit man of Bournemouth.

Gladly, no reports of female stewards clobbered by a flailing boot, but maybe a line about living in harmony for the father's speech at the Mostyn wedding reception on Saturday.

Bournemouth: (4-4-2): Forde; Bradbury, Gowling, Pearce, Cummings; Gradel (Marvin 89), Anderton, Cooper, Hollands; Kuffour, Vokes.
Subs: Pryce (g), Young, Ryan, Pitman.
Booked: Bradbury.
Goal: Vokes (55).

Crewe Alexandra (4-5-1): Williams; McCready, Baudet (Carrington 59), O'Donnell, Abbey; Morgan, Schumacher (Jones 76), Lunt, Roberts, Maynard; Pope
Subs: Cox, Moore, Fon-Williams (g).
Booked: none.

Referee: K Hill (Hertfordshire).

Sick note strikes the right note? Former England player Darren Anderton leads by example with a determined tackle on Crewe's Gary Roberts.

Pic courtesy of Michael Cunningham

POSTSCRIPT: *Jeff Mostyn invested more money in the club the following Tuesday when the administrator threatened to close it after both consortia failed to realise funds to buy Bournemouth. At press, he was still chairman and seeking a suitable business partner while negotiating new contracts for the players, who were still on half pay at the time.*

Though Bournemouth had far more of the possession and play, a 1-1 draw at Carlisle United was not sufficient to save the day. Even a victory would not have been enough since Cheltenham beat Doncaster Rovers. Still, Mostyn did attend his daughter's wedding, albeit with a 'live feed' in his ear provided by Radio Solent.

"I looked like some secret serviceman walking around the grounds," said Mostyn, who remains fearful that a 15-points penalty in the Leeds fashion could be imposed before a ball is kicked next season.

"The wedding was a huge success, I'm glad to report, even if there were mixed emotions. I made the father's speech half-an-hour after the game had ended but was able to present a shirt signed by all the players to my daughter so she will remember the day for various reasons as well. Mainly, though, it put things into perspective because we were all among family and friends and that's what counts. The football club had to come second, even though at times you wouldn't think that was the case."

Saturday, May 3

Nottingham Forest 3 Yeovil Town 2

City Ground

A win for Nottingham Forest and anything less than victory for Doncaster Rovers at Cheltenham Town will see the Garibaldi Reds sneak into second place and secure promotion on the last day of the season.

SOMEWHERE in the equation there should have been a beach. Sun, sea and sangria certainly, bleached blonds and glowing yellow sand soaking up the ebbing crystal blue tide.

Or at the very least, a crowded swimming pool with straw donkeys and hats and outrageously pink miniature umbrellas adorning equally exotic cocktails.

In the event, Nottingham Forest settled for the sun and a nervous sweat as they restored their Championship status after an absence of three years in the hitherto uncharted regions of football's third tier.

A merited but ultimately fraught 3-2 victory over Yeovil Town, ironically the side that overwhelmingly dumped them out of the semi finals of the play-offs a year ago, was greeted with joyous celebrations, a mixture of blessed relief and genuine excitement in daring to ponder that perhaps a corner had been turned at Forest. A downward spiral halted irrevocably.

Time will tell, of course, but with such merriment and celebration at the City Ground, the tenure of Brian Clough inevitably sprang readily to mind.

Above: It's over — a small step back to the big time for the little club that Cloughie transformed. Time will tell if it proves to be a giant one.

Pics courtesy of the Nottingham Evening Post

Below: Forest players, from left — Ian Breckin, Sammy Clinghan, Junior Agogo, Wes Morgan and Luke Chambers — cannot hide their delight, or tattoos.

At Derby County he received news that the club were First Division champions while holidaying with the squad in Cala Millor. Five turbulent years later, in 1977, he was in the same Majorcan resort with the Forest players when Wolverhampton Wanderers beat Bolton Wanderers. The 1-0 win for the visiting team denied Bolton third place in the Second Division so Forest held on to an automatic promotion that was the prelude to the club's unprecedented success, which included the First Division title and two European Cups in the ensuing three seasons.

A repeat performance in the near future is as likely as Robin Hood's resurrection in Sherwood Forest, but then ambitions have diminished appreciably since Clough's swagger held sway among the game's enduring elite.

Forest chairman Nigel Doughty, a supporter since he was in school uniform shorts and the man who has financed this latest slow-burn renaissance, insists the club is tilting at the top once again. Survival there, as Derby County, the deadly enemy down the A52 or Brian Clough Way, can confirm is an aspiration to be commended. Any notion of actually winning the Premier League or finishing above third bottom is simply entering the realms of fantasy, although winning the occasional game, or more than a one in 38 average, would have been nice for the Rams.

Doughty's track record, he was highly influential in the calamitous appointment of David Platt and did not invest in Paul Hart's young squad when it was most needed, may not be initially impressive, but clearly he has learned by his mistakes, among which must be Joe Kinnear, given the manager's job when Hart was sacked four years ago.

Now the venture capitalist can dream of reviving Forest's fortunes – to an extent at any rate.

"I don't really like using terms like embarrassment but it is embarrassing for a club of this stature to be in League

One," he said. "This has been my club since I was five or six and I have felt embarrassed that we have dropped into the third tier. I will still be a bit embarrassed until we are back in the Premier League because this is a Premier League club. We should be established at that level and pushing on to achieve things from there."

Colin Calderwood, the manager who was barracked just five weeks ago by around 3,000 fans who demanded he should be dismissed after defeat at Doncaster Rovers, should be the beneficiary of Doughty's hard-earned football wisdom as well as some considerable financial backing. The club's wage bill alone, around £7million per annum, is the envy of most Championship clubs.

Robert Earnshaw, the tooth-laden travelling man of that level, is a £2million target by all accounts, although his departure from Derby may herald the arrival of Kris Commons, one of Forest's most creative talents, at Pride Park.

"I don't think the ambition is anything to be scared of. When I took the job it was the best one that summer [2006] and not one to be fearful of," Calderwood said. "The expectancy lifts you and drives you on. To be the manager of a successful team here again next season in this city would probably take it to another level. We've now got to add the right characters and right amount of experience. We sat down and discussed the budget quite a while ago. We had a Plan A and a Plan B - and we'll certainly enjoy Plan A."

Six wins in seven games since that defeat at the Keepmoat Stadium have been crucial to Forest's – and Calderwood's – rosier future.

Local lads Julian Bennett, Commons and Lewis McGugan scored the first half goals that put Forest in the ascendancy, a pleasing homegrown talent that augurs well for progress. Jamie Peters and Andy Kirk replied, not enough however, and with Doncaster falling at the final hurdle at Cheltenham, Forest were up.

It is a matter of debate for how long and how far they can travel from here.

Lewis McGugan is congratulated after his goal secured a 3-1 lead for Forest. It seemed enough, and despite a few wobbles before the final whistle, it was.

Pic courtesy of the Nottingham Evening Post

Nottingham Forest (4-4-2): P Smith; Chambers (Breckin 73), Wilson, Morgan, Bennett; Perch (Agogo 65), McGugan, Cohen, Commons; Ormerod, (Davies 86), Tyson
Subs: Thornhill, McCleary.
Booked: McGugan
Goals: Bennett (12), Commons (18), McGugan (28)

Yeovil Town (4-4-2): Mildenhall; Peltier, Skiverton, Forbes, N Smith; Peters, Barry (Rose 79), Bircham, Williams (Kirk 68); Downes (Jones 84), Stewart
Subs: Guyett, Owusu.
Booked: Williams, Skiverton.
Goals: Peters (20), Kirk (75)

Referee: F Graham (Essex)

Right: Colin Calderwood cracks a smile at last – promotion delivered, job done and the Forest manager was magnanimous in victory, refusing to chastise those who had doubted his ability to steer the club to the Championship

Pic courtesy of the Nottingham Evening Post